# KIVIE KAPLAN

## A Legend

## in

## His Own Time

# KIVIE KAPLAN

# A Legend in His Own Time

*Edited by* Dr. S. Norman Feingold

*and*

Rabbi William B. Silverman

MCMLXXVI

Union of American Hebrew Congregations

NEW YORK

© Copyright, 1976 by the Union of American
Hebrew Congregations


Library of Congress Cataloging in Publication
Data
Main entry under title:

Kivie Kaplan: a legend in his own time.

   1. Kaplan, Kivie, 1904-1975.   2. Judaism
and social problems—Addresses, essays, lec-
tures.   3. National Association for the Advancement of Colored People.   I. Feingold, S.
Norman.          II. Silverman, William B.
E184.J5K55      296.6'1 [B]          76-2410
ISBN 0-8074-0006-8

Produced in the United States of America

# CONTENTS

# PREFACE

THIS volume is a loving and thoughtful recollection of the life of a remarkable man—Kivie Kaplan. Edited by two of his good friends—Dr. S. Norman Feingold and Rabbi William B. Silverman—it draws upon the memories of only a few of the many people whose lives Kivie affected so deeply. The writers include black leaders, rabbis, a United States senator, authors, social workers, members of his immediate family, and co-workers in great causes.

Together they have fashioned not a portrait—Kivie was too multifaceted and three-dimensional for that—but a mosaic of a rich and useful life as it was lived by a colorful and unforgettable human being. This is a worthy salute to a gallant fighter for social justice.

We are grateful to the editors for their perseverance; to Ralph Davis for his excellent guidance in this production; to Josette Knight for her great care in proofreading and editing the manuscript; to Cheryl Sortor and Liz Levine for their tireless assistance, and to Andor Braun, designer of the book.

But, of course, as the contributors point out—and as Kivie would have shouted from the housetops—the only true way to honor one's memory is to perpetuate the work of his hands. Accordingly, the NAACP and the UAHC—the two groups to which Kivie gave most lavishly of himself and his resources—have jointly established a *Kivie Kaplan Human Relations Fund.* In this living and enduring memorial, we will seek to encourage black-Jewish collaboration—nationally and in local communities—for the advancement of human rights and social justice. With funds generated by this project, young men and women will be trained as interns in the field of intergroup relations, hopefully to

vii

devote their life's work—as Kivie did—to the fulfillment of that biblical mandate, still so acutely relevant today: to proclaim liberty, affirm human dignity, and establish justice at the gates.

# KIVIE

# KAPLAN

## 1904-1975

# 1

# Two Friends Touch a Legend

## PART I

## *S. Norman Feingold*

\*

HOW do you write objectively about a long-time close friend, particularly if the friend was someone with whom you shared peak experiences, both of joy and sorrow?

How do you relate to a long-time friend who really cares and in whom you have complete confidence and trust? This, in itself, is a peak human experience.

Kivie Kaplan was already a legend in his own time when we became friends more than thirty years ago in Boston.

Kivie was born on April 1, 1904, in Boston. The date of his birth is as easy to recall as the man himself. Once you met Kivie Kaplan, you never forgot him. He had a unique personality with a rare mix of abilities, achievements, and interests.

One cannot describe Kivie without Emily. She is a lady in every sense of the word. Emily and Kivie were happily married for almost fifty years. Cousins, they fell in love during the first year of high school and knew from the beginning that someday they would get married. Throughout the years they together experienced in depth great things of both joy and sorrow. They were so much more than just another married couple. They reinforced one another. They blended together. They reached unusual heights as parents, grandparents, and great-grandparents. They were blessed with the solid marriages of two devoted daughters, Sylvia Grossman and Jean Green. Their only son, Edward Kaplan, a professor of history, gave them deep pride and joy.

Emily is a quiet, somewhat shy person, at least as compared to Kivie. She is always impeccably dressed and carries herself with dignity. She is very much a person in her own right, knows what is going on at all times, and participates in many activities, especially when the chips are down. The Kaplan family life style was always in the best of taste whether it was

DR. S. NORMAN FEINGOLD *is national director of the B'nai B'rith Career and Counseling Services and a past president of the American Personnel and Guidance Association.*

3

in flower arrangement or furniture, but it also reflected the kind of home that was lived in and enjoyed. Emily embroiders, whenever possible, unusually beautiful napkins and table-cloths for the trousseaus of her grandchildren. She, as did Kivie, "sheps much naches" from their children and grand-children. All are in the forefront of philanthropy and social justice movements in the context of their faith.

When needs were evidenced, the team of Emily and Kivie responded with heart and mind. She could and did bring a balance wheel to Kivie Kaplan's tremendous talents, energies, and drives.

How do you relate to a friend whose son says at an early age, "Dad, I need a larger allowance," and when Kivie, in reply, tells him he is already getting an allowance that is probably much too high, remarks, "But, Dad, if you give me a larger allowance, I will be able to give more to charity"? Thousands of people of all races, colors, and creeds were helped by Kivie. Many remain anonymous, including num-bers of college graduates all over the country.

I have seen his two daughters and his son over the years mature in so many subtle ways, as they came under the strong influence of a famous father. Power was a sacred trust to Kivie and was not to be abused.

It seems like yesterday and yet like the distant past when Kivie Kaplan called me at my office one day many years ago. He wanted to know more about what I was doing to help youths and adults in the area of counseling and selective placement. He had read about me in the local newspapers. We had lunch at the then Colonial Tanning Company offices. Even then, Kivie was a key leader in the Boston area. I greatly appreci-ated his genuine outreach and concern and looked forward with great enthusiasm to our getting together. From the first time we met I was drawn to him. There was a charisma, a magnetism, and an authenticity which one felt immediately. Friendly and relaxed, he was on top of the situation. He made me and others there feel important. The luncheon was an extra good one, although it had been prepared for so many people at one time. The session was an exciting one with Kivie almost acting in the role of moderator.

The dining room at the Colonial Tanning Company in Boston is forever etched in my memory. The truly delicious meals, planned by a home economist, were complimentary for all employees, executive and support staff alike. People worked and ate together. The story is human.

I attended many lunches there. They were always learning experiences. People who were luncheon guests were in various shapes, sizes, and colors from near and far, but they all had something to say and give. It was like a great big grab bag when you visited Kivie. You never knew what key personality you would meet.

Enjoyable as a visit was to Colonial Tanning or other businesses under the direction of Kivie, one could readily see his no-nonsense approach to business, a thrust that separated the men from the boys. In those days, and often since, Kivie introduced me as his personal psychologist. As a psychologist I have been trained in how to try to be objective, in how to try to separate fact from fancy, data from emotion, and the person from the performance. As I write this chapter, I think of how the lives of the Kaplans and the Feingolds meshed together in so many self-actualizing ways, not only for ourselves but also for our families. However, even in such an exact science as physics, the act of measurement changes the data.

How do you relate to a man whom you have known so well, who always has stood up and been counted no matter how painful the issue? I can recall the thick mud and his deep concern at Resurrection City in Washington, D.C., when we walked there together. Here was a man who was warm and at times emotional but who knew that when the chips are down one must keep his cool and do what is right.

I was with Kivie in Los Angeles at an NAACP convention when an attempt was made against his life. A tall, muscular man dressed as a priest attacked him. Kivie kept his cool and the man was overcome. Moreover, Kivie remained at the convention as if the incident were merely another daily occurrence. For many years I worked with him at other NAACP conventions to help hundreds of black youths with tremendous potential who needed counseling and financial assistance to make their dreams come true. Kivie paid my expenses to attend the conventions and I gave up vacation time. Each convention is also highlighted by the annual coveted Kivie Kaplan Life Membership Awards. They are given to NAACP branches that make outstanding contributions to the life membership programs each year. These awards are presented annually at the life membership luncheon during the NAACP convention. The life membership program initiated by Kivie Kaplan now has Sammy Davis, Jr., as its national chairman; it has enrolled more than 53,000 persons so far. There are, moreover, sixty life members in the Kaplan family, spanning four generations. The first of the fifth generation to become a life member was born recently. Many of the life members who live in foreign countries were secured by Kivie during his travels abroad. I was with Kivie in Washington, D.C., when the NAACP honored Frank Wills, the guard whose quick thinking and action led to the arrest of the Watergate burglars. Kivie's membership and involvement in the NAACP went back some forty-two years.

Youths at these conventions hungered for knowledge and for someone who really cared and could make a difference in their lives. Years later, numbers of these young people came back and told me about their triumphs, struggles, and achievements. Kivie was there with interest and concern for them. He was always available when one could not go any further without added help and encouragement.

I have also been present when Kivie was interviewed by a friendly or hostile reporter. As president of the NAACP, he was always prepared to handle the latest developments.

Kivie was a truly pious man whose friends spanned every segment of Jewish religious and organizational life. A trustee of both Temple Emanuel and Temple Israel of Boston, he was also an honorary member of a Congregational church.

It was my good fortune to be present at the dedication of the Emily and Kivie Kaplan Social Action Center in Washington, D.C., where the Holy Torah was presented to President John F. Kennedy. It was a moment of unusual beauty and serenity. There were tears in many people's eyes, including those of Emily and Kivie.

I was with Kivie in New York at the 1973 Union of American Hebrew Congregations convention, the one marked by the death of Rabbi Maurice N. Eisendrath. Kivie was a good friend of Maurice Eisendrath with whom he worked closely as vice-chairman of the UAHC Board of Trustees and member of the Executive Committee.

His community achievements spanned the gamut of the American voluntary way, whether it was service on the board of directors of a hospital or helping new Americans find jobs as a first step in rebuilding their lives. He was sophisticated, worldly wise, and traveled. He knew of much hypocrisy and double standards, but he remained an optimist by temperament and conviction. He was a people-centered person who was not only keenly interested and involved in his Jewish heritage and its survival but in the rights of his fellow human beings everywhere. Every man was his brother. When Kivie Kaplan said "brother" or "sister" to another human being he meant what the word implies. Kivie was a practical man with a homespun philosophy that encompassed for him the complexities of our lives in the searching seventies.

For many years Emily and Kivie wintered at Safety Harbor Spa in Florida. Kivie was probably the best known of the many hundreds of guests who came to that resort each year. Friends called or were invited to break bread with Emily and Kivie. Some were people who were once afraid to stand up and be counted. They do so now because Kivie was a convincing person, whether selling a life membership in the NAACP or Israel Bonds.

Kivie received hundreds of awards from hundreds of different organizations. Years ago there was an ego room at his home with plaques, keys, and other awards, tokens of various people's love and respect. And at the same time in his beautiful home in Newton, Massachusetts, there was a large storehouse of all kinds of goodies, exotic foods, toys, mementos, and hundreds of books for friends. Even the young people had their particular spot, for one room contained a large soda fountain with all the fixings. Kivie related to people of all ages at all levels of education, training, and status.

He enjoyed the honors, but none of them changed his passion for justice or his way of life. The work had to continue or ground gained soon could be lost. Kivie was a realist in whatever he did. A few honors taken from the files at random are: T. Kenyon Holly Award for outstanding humanitarian service in civic, cultural, and philanthropic fields; Temple Reyim Brotherhood Man of the Year Award; Wilfred S. Stachenfeld Award; awards from the National Association for the Advancement of Colored People, Associated Jewish Philanthropies and Combined Jewish Appeal, Jewish Chautauqua Society, Union of American Hebrew Congregations; Modern Community Developers' first annual Averell Harriman Equal Housing Opportunity Award. He has been referred to often in books, magazines, newspapers and is also listed in various volumes of *Who's Who*, including *Who's Who in World Jewry*.

Kivie Kaplan, who never graduated from college, received honorary doctorate degrees from Portia Law School, Wilberforce University, Lincoln University, Hebrew Union College—Jewish Institute of Religion, Saints College, and Edward Waters College. At least two books have been dedicated to him and his wife. Kivie loved learning and people who love learning. He was open, flexible, willing to listen and be changed or to try to change those with whom he disagreed. He probably knew more Orthodox, Conservative, Reconstructionist, and Reform rabbis than any other lay community

leader in the country. When he traveled, he spoke at synagogues and temples, as well as at churches of various per-
suasions.

The more you trusted and turned to Kivie, the more he
emerged as a person who had lasting values. Every person is
important. Every person can make a contribution. Kivie often
stated that money doesn't talk, it screams; but used wisely, it
brings about needed changes. His contributions have allowed
the B'nai B'rith Career and Counseling Services to publish
many thousands of career briefs on the Peace Corps and
VISTA that have attracted thousands of young people to service
on behalf of their country. Hundreds of representatives and
senators congratulated Kivie on this worthwhile project.

How do you summarize Kivie Kaplan? What does it
mean to say that he was a man just over the age of three score
and ten, 5 feet 9 inches? He was a pleasant-looking man who
seemed taller and heavier than he was. He dressed casually and
loved good food well prepared, particularly fish. He constantly
watched his diet under the careful eye of Emily, who tried to
see that he stayed within prescribed limits. Kivie's "Keep
Smiling" cards printed in dozens of languages were great ice-
breakers even with those who sharply disagreed with him.
These cards are found all over the world. I saw one glued to a
counter in a small cafe in Beersheba, Israel.

Kivie was a pleasant, extroverted, achievement-oriented
man who at all times was ready to listen and in turn told it
as he saw it. His concern was always for the underdog. He
was disarmingly bright, quick on the draw, and often came
to the heart of the problem while others still skirted the true
issues.

He was always a heavyset man, but able to move quickly
on his feet. He was action-oriented but had a great deal of
frustration tolerance as long as one was pointing in the appropriate direction. To the best knowledge of this writer, no one
has sat on as many boards of directors of colleges and universities, or governing bodies of other agencies for community

and religious welfare. For Kivie Kaplan was always ahead of his time—whether in running his industry with profit sharing and free meals for everyone, or initiating a foundation as part of the leather industry which would help needy employees. Here was a man who left his indelible imprint on every board of directors or committee he served on. I recall when a board of directors were thinking for years in terms of a work-adjustment center for the handicapped. Kivie heard the story. The community needs were outlined. Kivie told the story in new terms to the appropriate people, and the rehabilitation facility came into being without further delay.

A tremendous correspondent, Kivie kept abreast of everything he initiated or helped to initiate. He rarely forgot, and he was exceedingly well organized. Through personal visits, phone calls, and letters, he touched base with people all over the world. During the Israeli Yom Kippur war Kivie was on the phone to Israel in a much needed helping capacity. He retained old friends and continually made new ones. He felt a sense of destiny and had the good fortune of continually grabbing a fistful of tomorrow. Many of the things he broached or talked about years ago have been ultimately adopted both in organizations and business life. Wealth and power too often corrupt, but not Kivie Kaplan, a man who gave untold sums to make this a better world in which to live. As a philanthropist, he did not merely give funds but sought to make people independent, to help them make decisions so they could live a full and satisfying life.

At times Kivie overwhelmed people by his sheer energy and persuasion in a cause. One almost had to run while Kivie walked, for anything in relation to people was important. Kivie was a humble man. He was not dazzled by wealth, honor, nor the famous people he met. There were always items that he could chat about on a level that was interesting to all concerned.

Kivie's dedication to service was a twenty-four-hour job. He rarely lost the opportunity of following up a lead to help, for he believed that every person should be able to live in dignity and respect.

Kivie used to drive his Cadillac down to Florida. On the way to and from he would speak with many friends, particularly rabbis, as well as NAACP groups, church and synagogue gatherings. He was a great attraction, and people would come from long distances to hear his message. He would judge an audience and react intuitively in a way that added meaning and a message. He had the car stocked with books and goodies for his friends whom he stopped to see en route.

Even though one can be helpful to people who act contrary to what one would expect from a good turn, Kivie never lost faith in his fellow humans. I recall a number of occasions when Kivie and I were in the state prison together (as visitors!). He worked on a rehabilitation program to help Jewish inmates before and after discharge. When inmates were released from prison, he trusted them. Even when the trust was misplaced, Kivie would continue to help others for in changing one person, as Hillel so aptly stated, you have changed the world. Each day offered more opportunities for Kivie to help others.

I heard Kivie Kaplan speak eloquently in so many places in this country, including Martha's Vineyard, where he used to summer for more than thirty years. Here was a man impelled by a cause, who made a noticeable difference for thousands of people of all colors, races, and creeds.

I can recall many luncheons and dinners in both unknown and outstanding places with the famous and the not-so-famous whom Kivie gathered around him from all over the United States and the world. I can recall the Jacksonville, Florida, auditorium filled to capacity as Kivie Kaplan, Robert St. John, and I received honorary doctorate degrees. The evening before, key officials and faculties of college and community got together to celebrate the upcoming graduation. The center of attention was Kivie Kaplan.

Kivie was much more complex than may have been apparent to the casual observer. His span of interests was exceedingly high, but at all times he remained people-centered. This was what kept the man going and furnished the fuel that allowed him to make such significant changes in so many people's lives. He knew them all as individuals. He knew waiters and janitors, as well as representatives, senators, and college presidents, and he related to all of them at an appropriate level. He bridged the gap in relating to people no matter what their age, background, or life style.

I recall interesting evenings with Kivie and Emily and their friends chatting with the late S. Ralph Harlow, who was so influential in Kivie's life. Ralph Harlow was the only man I ever met who always read the menu from right to left, worrying about the cost, no matter how often Kivie would insist on the contrary. Ralph would say over and over, "I really do like hamburger." A retired professor of theology at Smith College and a prolific author, Ralph was always a great inspiration to Kivie as well as to so many others who knew him.

Kivie was an exceptionally bright person who was disarmingly pleasant and unassuming. He listened and remembered. He was thinking ahead. Moreover, he had an uncanny ability of being on the right side in important issues. His quick judgments were often the same as those made by others who had been deliberating over them for long periods of time. He could quickly distinguish foe, fraud, and friend, for his gut reactions were exceptionally perceptive. Kivie trusted himself.

Kivie still found time to relax with friends and relatives. He did a great deal of reading in a wide variety of magazines and newspapers. He shared his reading and news with his friends and had a part-time secretary who helped keep him up to date. He knew what the bigots were saying and doing, for Kivie Kaplan was a constant object of their hatred. Their activities only sparked his greater commitment to his fellow human being.

Books and pamphlets are distributed by the thousands so as to change behavior with a thrust toward social justice.

Nevertheless, Kivie always had his feet on the ground and reminded you that for some it is too late. We must wait for some bigots to die before certain changes can take place. Kivie's enthusiasm was contagious. He was anxious that we not continue to let the "bland lead the bland."

He probably gave away more books than are in the library of a relatively large city. He believed in what the poet Milton so aptly expressed, "A good book is the precious life blood of a master spirit." Thousands of scholarly and popular books on hundreds of topics have been given to friends and colleagues. People knew that if he offered them a book (usually with the autograph of the author), it carried with it the obligation to read it and chat about it when they got together. Untold numbers of books have reached print only with his help. One author, at least, in this book got his start through the generosity and encouragement of Kivie.

The man, Kivie, was a great illustration that the whole is far greater than the sum of its parts. Much that Kivie was is revealed in this book. There was, however, still much more to Kivie Kaplan. Many more chapters not yet written are in the archives of the Union of American Hebrew Congregations and the Armistad Research Center, Dillard University, in New Orleans, but we trust enough has been presented to insure the validity of the title of this book — *Kivie Kaplan: A Legend in His Own Time.* It was Zusia, the chasidic rabbi, who said, "When I shall face the celestial tribunal I shall not be asked why I was not Abraham, Jacob, or Moses. I shall be asked why I was not Zusia." Kivie Kaplan knew his identity, for he remained Kivie Kaplan at all times.

Kivie often said, "I will wear out, but never rust out." And thus, in his last years, Kivie did more than he should have in spite of his repeated attempts to cut down his manifold service activities. "Don't be a dead hero" was his advice, although too often Kivie did not follow his own motto. It was not easy for a man of Kivie's energies, talents, and drives to slow down when so much more had to be done. However, he was leaving a good many boards of directors and committees where he was the driving force. He was reorganizing his priorities, but in spite of cutting down he put more time and energy in volunteer service than many executives do in their jobs and careers.

The writers of the various chapters of this book were selectively chosen for they are people who significantly touched Kivie's life. They are all well known in their own right. The author of each chapter has written about Kivie from the perspective in which he saw him. Each author presents a facet of the man he knew from where he viewed him and in a significant portion of his life. The meaning and common thrusts of the chapters are summarized by my friend and colleague, Rabbi William B. Silverman, coeditor of this book. For us, it has been a labor of love.

To the authors and editors, Kivie offered a working model of just what one person can do to make this world a better place in which to live. This book, written by key leaders in many walks of life, we hope will stimulate others to do what Kivie has done or to take up the torch for social justice. We believe in the effects of successful models for changing human behavior. Kivie Kaplan stood as one living model that others may wish to emulate.

Kivie spent his time wisely and well. Time to him was an ingredient that was to be filled with meaningful activities. It was not to be idly wasted whether he be on a plane, car, or train. He often wrote himself notes and followed through, and got more out of an hour's time than any other person I have known. Kivie's style and timing plus creative action equaled results.

In career guidance we often ask five questions:

Who are you?
Where have you been?
Where are you going?
How are you going to get there?
Why?

Kivie answered these questions and lived a life that defied the imagination. There was always something to add. Kivie was a man who always found time for family and friends. He was aptly described by Rabbi Herman Pollack in the chapter he has written as the man with a great heart.

In closing, let me tell the following story which sums up Kivie's day-to-day philosophy: A gardener was told by his employer to plant a certain shrub. "But sir, it won't bloom for a hundred years." "Then plant it at once. We have no time to lose."

This was the wide, wide world of Kivie Kaplan.

# 1

# Two Friends Touch a Legend

## PART II

### William B. Silverman

*

ON MARCH 16, 1958, a dynamite explosion ripped off the front of the Jewish Community Center of Nashville, Tennessee. Shortly after the explosion my wife, Pearl, received an ominous telephone call: "This is Captain Gordon of the Confederate Underground. We have just dynamited the Jewish Community Center. Next we are going to shoot down in cold blood Federal Judge William E. Miller and next your nigger-loving husband!"

At that time I was serving as the senior rabbi of Temple Ohabai Sholom and was active in the effort to implement the Supreme Court decision on the integration of the public schools.

The families of four black children had requested permission to enroll them in the first grade of a Nashville public school. Despite legal efforts to delay integration, Judge Miller had just issued a legal order to permit black children to enroll in what had been a segregated school.

What followed was a nightmare to me and my family: anonymous calls, poison pen letters, dead rats thrown on the porch. There were threats of smashed windows and dynamiting the temple, maiming our children, murdering the "nigger-loving rabbi." I obtained a permit to carry a gun, and the police and state militia were stationed at our home for twenty-four hours a day.

It was during this time that I received a long-distance call from Boston. The voice said: "My name is Kivie Kaplan. I admire you for your fight for justice and I want you, your wife, and children to come stay with Emily and me in Boston until this blows over."

After thanking Mr. Kaplan for his generous hospitality, his consideration, and concern, I told him I was remaining in Nashville to continue the fight against segregation and injustice.

---

RABBI WILLIAM SILVERMAN *is the rabbi emeritus of Congregation B'nai Jehudah in Kansas City, Missouri.*

Kivie Kaplan then made a statement that I regarded somewhat dubiously. He said: "From this time on, you are my friend. You will receive either a letter or a telephone call from me every week of my life."

Although my heart was warmed by his encouragement and support, I must confess that I didn't take this very seriously. I was wrong. Every week since that date I received either a letter or a telephone call from Kivie Kaplan.

The name of Kivie Kaplan was not unfamiliar to me. I had seen some of his cards stating, "Keep Smiling," with a somewhat sentimental poem on brotherhood by S. Ralph Harlow on the back of the card. My feeling was that this was probably a very eccentric gentleman, a little peculiar, a man of wealth who had to find some way of getting his name before the public by way of ego nurturing. Again, I couldn't have been more wrong. He may have been eccentric in the sense of being a unique personality, but there was nothing ludicrous or publicity-seeking about Kivie Kaplan.

Through the years I began to know Kivie and Emily and felt not only a deep personal affection for both of them but I met their children and grandchildren and was awed by the devotion of Kivie and Emily to their family and to each other. Seeing him and being with him throughout the years, my appreciation of him was enhanced by further knowledge of his contributions to and leadership of not only secular organizations but also religious organizations, primarily the Union of American Hebrew Congregations whose president was then Maurice N. Eisendrath.

Throughout his life, Rabbi Eisendrath worked with dedicated zeal for social justice. His prophetic voice resounded throughout the world demanding righteousness, exhorting his people to social action in behalf of the afflicted and the oppressed, summoning men and women of conscience to compassion and concern. It was Maurice Eisendrath who designated Kivie Kaplan as his representative at the Conference of Presidents in Israel in 1972. Kivie Kaplan had great admiration for Maurice Eisendrath and found a co-worker in the field of human relations and a partner in the effort to secure justice, not only for Jews, but for blacks and for those of every faith and every race.

Both men appreciated the admonition of the Torah that commands: "Justice, justice shall ye pursue." Kivie Kaplan and Maurice Eisendrath could understand and empathize with the teachings of the rabbis, asking why the word *justice* is repeated twice. The sages answered: "It is repeated twice to teach justice for those of your faith and those who are not of your faith, justice for those who are of your people and those who are not of your people." Just means must be used to seek just ends. Justice had to reach out and be equally applicable to all people. Justice had to be seen through the perspective of universality and as the force that moves God's children in the direction of divinity.

### Who Was Kivie Kaplan?

A friend who recently returned from Israel said that the taxi driver had given him a little card on which was written "Keep Smiling" in Hebrew and in English and signed "Kivie Kaplan." He asked me: "Who is Kivie Kaplan?"

In 1971, Kivie was speaking in the area of Kansas City, Missouri, and my wife and I invited him and Emily to be guests in our home. We didn't see too much of Kivie because he was meeting with officials of the NAACP and addressing groups in small communities adjacent to Kansas City. He would come back to our home to sleep and rest a little. During that time he received a sad telephone call from a rabbi who had just lost a child, another from a rabbi who had just been ousted from his job, and yet another call from a rabbi asking about a pulpit possibility. The long-distance calls were coming with great rapidity from rabbis seeking his advice, financial help, and moral support. In some cases Kivie was financially helpful.

In all cases he was humanly and emotionally supportive. How did he inspire such confidence in men and women? What was there about this man that would motivate people to turn to him in their need? Why was it and is it important for me and Norman Feingold, another very dear friend, to do a book on Kivie Kaplan, convinced that he had become a legend in his time?

While Kivie was an ample man physically, robust and heavy set, how do you put flesh on his personality? How do you portray with words the smile on his lips, the gentle twinkle in his eye, his look of concern, the tenderness of his love for his wife? Despite the difficulty, those who have written chapters for this volume have endeavored to do so, and the reader, we hope, will be able to create his own image of a truly great man.

Who was Kivie Kaplan? He was a man who ordered from authors hundreds of books on social justice and human rights. Any visitor to his home usually left with a virtual literary CARE package in addition to sweets and goodies. There were little bags filled with autographed books pertaining to rights for the blacks, Jewish wisdom, biographies, and civil liberties. In addition there would be pretzels, carmel corn, and other little gifts.

Who was Kivie Kaplan? A man who loved his wife ("the Bobee"), his children, his sons-in-law, his daughter-in-law, his grandchildren, and his great-grandson. Kivie was on the telephone, writing letters, taking his family with him on travels—but even more, being supportive in any family crisis or illness. As husband, father, grandfather, and great-grand-father, he was always there when needed.

Who was Kivie Kaplan? Having dinner on his itinerary southward with rabbis and lay people who had problems because of controversies with their congregations, constituents, or jobs. What mixtures of personalities were present when you had dinner with Kivie and Emily? Blacks, Christians, Jews, scholars, porters, taxi drivers, as a beaming Kivie and Emily hosted the dinner.

Who was Kivie Kaplan? With a dictating machine in almost every room of his house he dictated letters to friends, to the hospitalized, to ministers and rabbis, to presidents of colleges and universities — letters to almost every country in the world, letters in support of Israel, letters expressing concern and compassion, but always the familiar blue print on the envelope and the typed letter offering love and support, signed "Kivie." (When I visited with him in his home I really expected to find a dictaphone in every bathroom, too.)

Who was Kivie Kaplan? The man who anticipated the "Black Is Beautiful" movement and told blacks a long time before it became a cultural trend to be proud of being black. He reminded them of their royal heritage, of their human dignity, of the need to make something of themselves by getting an education, by reinforcing or creating the conviction that they are significant, meaningful, and needed in our American culture.

Who was Kivie Kaplan? A smiling supersalesman of ideals who distributed blue, brown, and red neckties with the scale-of-justice design and a little note to friends suggesting that they wear this tie to remind themselves of the fight for justice.

Who was Kivie Kaplan? The fund raiser who went to black colleges and sought money for their support when they were in financial trouble; the quiet man who was present at almost every major fundraising drive for Jewish causes.

Who was Kivie Kaplan? The lay rabbi who helped conduct the religious services at a little Jewish congregation in Vineyard Haven. Arriving home he was surrounded by friends, disciples, members of the NAACP, and strangers who just dropped in to meet him and chat with him and who invariably left with an "I care" package.

Who was Kivie Kaplan? A gourmet who loved to eat but had to curtail his diet. Every once in a while he impishly afforded himself a treat by eating lobster in Vineyard Haven. First, however, he had to go into the kitchen to talk to the cooks, the waiters, and waitresses, inquiring of the owner about the forthcoming marriage of his daughter, making phone calls to physicians and specialists when their children were ill or a wife or a husband needed special medical attention—and usually footing the bill.

Kivie Kaplan didn't fit into any category or stereotype. His unique personality precluded the possibility of any precise typing. I do not believe that it was the incident of his seeing in Miami a sign reading "No Jews or Dogs Allowed" that really prompted him to begin his career of concern or that motivated him to go beyond himself to serve the cause of the black people. This may have in some sense sparked his devotion to social action. It may have aroused the potential of compassion to a structured dedication to causes. A study of his history indicates that he was always concerned about other human beings and just in his dealings with his business associates and his fellow human beings.

## The Paradox and the Paradigm

How do you begin to label such a man? He was not a scholar, but he furthered scholarship with his means and his enthusiasm. He was not a polished or professional speaker, and yet he traveled east, west, north, and south speaking for a cause. He was wealthy, yet he devoted himself to the poor and to the oppressed.

He was a paradigm and sometimes a paradox, exemplifying throughout his life what Karl Menninger calls the "Vital Balance." Let me illustrate.

Kivie hated to fight, but he persisted in battling and struggling for social justice. He was not a physician, yet he gave strength and financial support to the Jewish Memorial Hospital and other medical institutions and hospitals. He was white, but as the president of the NAACP he fought and worked as desperately, as persistently for black rights

as he did for the rights of his own race and his own people.

Kivie Kaplan loved praise and yet was embarrassed to
hear it. One evening I was with Kivie and Emily and a group
of his friends and I was telling them how much I admired and
respected Kivie, enumerating dramatically some of the things
he had done. I looked over at Kivie. His eyes were closing.
Soon he fell fast asleep even as I was praising him. Kivie may
have slept during the time when others praised him but he
was wide awake and alert when there was a human need, a
human being to be served, a cause to be strengthened, an act
of injustice to be rectified, a lonely soul to be supported and
nurtured with friendship. Cordial, smiling, and genial, he
possessed a mind that was incisive, an unbending will, and
an undaunted spirit. Up to his seventy-first year, he was still
smiling, still working, and still serving. With Kivie there was
always tomorrow and a myriad of tomorrows stretching
toward infinity.

One of the outstanding leaders of the Reform movement,
he was a member of the boards of trustees of Conservative
and Orthodox synagogues, supporting institutions and projects
sponsored by the Conservative and Orthodox movements in
the United States and in Israel.

He was the proud great-grandfather who took out a life
membership for his great-grandson, Joshua Adam, in the
NAACP and a life membership in the Jewish Chautauqua
Society of the National Federation of Temple Brother-
hoods.

Writing a critique of such a man is not easy because he
was complex and yet profoundly simple. Eminently practical
and down to earth, he was wed to poetry and music. Even
though he did not play a musical instrument, he loved symphony
concerts. Although tone deaf, he seldom missed a songfest
at Vineyard Haven. He would find it difficult to distinguish
between a kazoo and a bassoon, yet there was ever a harmony
in his life, a music that sang and resounded with a symphony

of life and love. Even though he never wrote a single line of poetry, his life symbolized a poetry that transcends words. He was a people person. His was a poetry of action, the expression of a sensitive soul reaching out to love and be loved. His works and words bespoke a vocabulary of concern and a cadence of compassion.

## A Bit of a Priest — A Bit of a Prophet

In the Jewish tradition there was always a tension between the priest and the prophet, between form and function, between ritual and righteousness. Kivie Kaplan was a deeply religious man. He was a pious man. There was seldom a Friday night he was not attending some worship service, whether Orthodox, Conservative, or Reform, whether in Boston, Tampa, Vineyard Haven, New Orleans, or Los Angeles. While not a strict traditionalist, his home reflected Jewish tradition and the observance of the Sabbath, the festivals, and the Holy Days. He was a *"K'lal Yisraelnik"* who loved all Jews and served all Jewish causes. In the most exalted sense he regarded himself as a member of "a kingdom of priests and a holy people," a man who saw Jews without labels or demarcations.

According to Jewish legend there are thirty-six persons unknown in every age and every generation and the world is saved because of their piety, virtue, and holiness. These people are called *"lamed vavniks."* Here was a *"lamed vavnik"* driving a Cadillac, a *"lamed vavnik"* distributing "I Care" packages. Here was an enthusiastic *"lamed vavnik"* expressing his love with a card, "Keep Smiling."

One need only read the Book of Leviticus, chapter 19, called the "Holiness Code," to learn that Kivie fulfilled the requisites of holiness. He was not an ascetic who isolated himself from society, eating herbs and grass, and spending his days in prayer, meditation, and eschatological speculation.

Kivie was always this-worldly, keeping the Sabbath and following the admonition to provide for the poor and for the stranger. He refused to accept the negative admonition, "Thou shalt not oppress thy neighbor or rob him," but insisted that positive action must be taken to help and serve your neighbor. Here was the *chasid* who exemplified the command of the "Holiness Code":

> Thou shalt not respect the person of the poor nor favor the person of the mighty. Thou shalt not go up and down as a tale bearer among thy people. Neither shalt thou stand idly by the blood of thy neighbor. Thou shalt not hate thy brother in thy heart. Thou shalt surely rebuke thy neighbor [for his indifference and passivity] and not bear sin because of him. Thou shalt not take vengeance nor bear any grudge against the children of thy people. Thou shalt love thy neighbor as thyself.

This is the Jewish definition of holiness, and according to this definition Kivie Kaplan lived a life of holiness and practiced holiness every day of his beautiful life.

Kivie's son Edward was a disciple of Abraham Joshua Heschel, who once said that all of life may be measured in moments of holiness. Edward loved Abraham Joshua Heschel and was an admiring disciple. Kivie Kaplan also respected Abraham Joshua Heschel but, even more, he attempted to make every moment of his life a moment of holiness by going beyond himself to those in need, to his fellow human beings crying out of the depths, to those who were oppressed and without hope.

While he fulfilled the requirements of priestly piety, he was the quiet but active prophet fighting injustice against any of God's children anywhere. Kivie Kaplan was not an angry man. He did not regard himself as a mouthpiece of or spokesman for divinity. He saw himself as an advocate of action who had to follow the admonition set forth by the prophet Micah: "To do justly, to love mercy, and to walk humbly with his God." His genial smile and composure were ruffled and disturbed only by injustice against human beings. Even his anger was expressed with mild annoyance and renewed determination to fight injustice with quiet resolve. He didn't like to criticize or speak against others. He could find many excuses to justify the behavior of even those who had been his severest critics. He adamantly refused to make a distinction between function and form. He believed that the form must lead to the function, that prayer must lead to positive action, that Jewishness is not limited to ritual observance but rather that ritual observance must galvanize him into a concern that is expressed through social action.

The need to offer a book about Kivie Kaplan has been almost a compulsion of the editors of this volume because to us he was the living example of the highest values of the Jewish faith that aspires up the mountaintop to the place where God may be seen, a faith of deed and not creed, a faith that committed him to action and asserted that we most beautifully and reverently demonstrate our love of God by serving God's children.

It was a Kivie Kaplan who could echo the sentiments of the sages who taught that when people appear before the throne of judgment they are not asked whether they observed ritual or even whether they believed in God but rather they must respond to the question: "Have you dealt ethically, faithfully, and morally with your fellow human beings?"

In another sense, Kivie was concerned with that which is definitively Jewish and yet he went beyond the Jews to the whole family of humankind. There he was passing out "Keep Smiling" cards to waitresses and waiters, taxi drivers and busboys, asking, "Are you a member of the NAACP? If not, why not?" He once said to me: "I can't do it all but I'd like to do something. I would like to be more concerned about the injustices that are done to the American Indians and Mexican Americans, the Japanese and Chinese Americans, but I'm afraid that I would dissipate my energies and efforts, so I'm concentrating upon doing a little to correct the great injustices done to the blacks."

With unbelievable drive, energy, and enthusiasm the indefatigable Kivie traveled, spoke, wrote, organized as he proceeded with his dedication to justice for the black people. He favored positive and affirmative action in making up for the years when the blacks were exploited and deprived of their legal rights and civil liberties. He stood forth to protest against those who insisted that the blacks are anti-Semitic and dangerous to American Jews, pointing out the negligible percentage of blacks who are involved in anti-Semitic movements. He declared with quiet demeanor that there are certainly more anti-Semites among the whites than there are among the blacks, and, even if there are anti-Semites among the blacks, we must not halt or desist in our efforts to show them the light, too, and to help dissipate their anti-Semitism. "We do not help them by being against them or hating them," he said.

Maintaining that busing is an equality and justice issue and not just a transportation issue, that fear is the reason for the reluctance of some people to accept busing, he spoke gently but firmly: "The bigot who can't sleep at night because he's afraid his daughter or son is going to marry a Negro is one of the problems. He's not right. In the words of the late Reverend Martin Luther King, Jr., 'We want to be the white man's brother and not his brother-in-law.' "

Frank Wills was a security guard at the Watergate office building. He is now a security guard without a job. His careful attention to duty helped to expose the Watergate scandal, but today he is unable to find meaningful work. Why? Rejected out of fear? Discrimination? For what reason is this particular man in this particular situation right now? I can recall vividly during the summer of 1973 when my wife and I were vacationing in Vineyard Haven, Kivie Kaplan was making plans with his grandson Barry to take him to Washington, D.C., on an occasion honoring Frank Wills. It was Kivie Kaplan who insisted this man not be forgotten, that the

NAACP honor Frank Wills. Kivie thought it important that his grandson meet a man who was conscientious about his work and whose sense of duty helped bring public attention to the scandal that shocked a nation.

Kivie, in his activities, moved from the intimate circle of his family to the Jewish people, his congregations, then beyond the Jewish people to those who were Christians. Muslims or Christians, blacks or whites, it didn't make any difference to Kivie who saw all people as children of God.

In our generation we have made rabbis surrogate Jews, the Jewish professionals, the religious functionaries who are supposed to learn Judaism, practice Judaism, love it and live it for Jewish laypersons. This is contrary to the spirit of a God-seeking, humanity-loving faith that has never placed the responsibility for social action upon its rabbinic leadership. Judaism insists that it is incumbent upon *every* Jew to be a member of a kingdom of priests and a holy people and not to wait for some messiah to appear supernaturally. Each individual is to regard himself or herself as a messiah, pledged to contribute to the betterment of society.

Kivie Kaplan was impelled by social conscience and a sense of compassion. His whole life was dedicated to the proposition that the religious ideals of Judaism must be applied to the living reality of human existence.

## The Secular and the Religious

Kivie made no distinction between the secular and the religious. True to the Jewish tradition, he saw himself as a layman who must learn and listen, who must act, speak, and maintain his covenant with his God—a Jew who must pray, practice, and not delegate or relegate his commitments to professional Jews. Consequently, he became involved with and made generous philanthropic contributions to both secular and religious organizations and institutions.

Hospitals, schools, community chests, synagogues, churches, black colleges and universities—all were of concern to Kivie Kaplan. How many black colleges and universities did he sustain not only with his own money but by raising funds from others? A man with a high school diploma, he had six honorary doctorates. Walking with the rich, the powerful, and the elite, he made it a point of seeking out the poor, the uneducated, and the afflicted.

I've seen many photographs of Kivie Kaplan: with Martin Luther King, Jr., Golda Meir, Senator Edward Brooke, Senator Edward Kennedy, and other notables. I've also seen pictures of Kivie Kaplan with just plain, ordinary people who occupy very plain positions and perform ordinary jobs.

He was criticized by blacks for remaining on as the white president of the NAACP. He was blamed by whites for obstructing the efforts of the blacks to do things for themselves and for taking too active a role in the leadership of the black movement. Kivie Kaplan was excoriated by those who criticized him for devoting so much time to the NAACP and who asked cryptically and sometimes bitterly why he didn't devote more time to Jewish causes. He was condemned despite the fact that he served on the board of Brandeis University and boards of synagogues, was vice-chairman of the Union of American Hebrew Congregations, supported the State of Israel, contributed to the Emily R. and Kivie Kaplan Religious Action Center of the UAHC of Washington, D.C., and helped establish a center for the World Union for Progressive Judaism in Jerusalem. The peripatetic priest and prophet traveled distances to meet with Rabbi Soloveitchik and other leaders of the Orthodox movement to plead for the rights of the Conservative and the Reform movements in Israel and in the United States. When Kivie was criticized or maligned for not being active enough in Jewish causes, he seldom defended himself or set forth the Jewish organizations and causes he had supported.

## Keep Smiling

When *Thunderbolt*, an anti-Semitic publication, caricatured him in the ugliest way, Kivie followed his own admonition of "Keep Smiling."

A man from Flushing, New York, who calls himself a concerned Jew, wrote to the Union of American Hebrew Congregations on February 1, 1973:

> How dare he and your organization deny reality and refuse to see that your sickening liberalism is putting the Jewish community of America in grave danger? .. Can't you people comprehend the seriousness of Jewish communities collapsing because of the influx of low-income crime ridden families under the guise of liberalism?
>
> Get off your backside and fight for Jewish rights or are you too ashamed to fight for your own people?
>
> Mr. Kaplan's statement is sickeningly reminiscent of similar ones exclaimed during the 1930's under the Hitler threat. . . . For crying out loud, it's about time you awakened to the fact that you are Jews first, and the Jewish rights and needs must be foremost and upmost.

Kivie read it and kept smiling.


## Why Don't You Help Your Fellow Jews?

I once asked Kivie to send me a list of the Jewish causes he served. He responded: "Not one of us does nearly enough in behalf of Jews and Judaism — so I'm not boasting. However, I do try to serve in some ways."

Here listed are some of the facilities he and Emily have supported, most of which bear his family name:

Admissions Office at Newton-Wellesley Hospital

Emily R. and Kive Kaplan Family Building of the Jewish Memorial Hospital

Emily R. and Kivie Kaplan Lincoln Hall at Brandeis University

Emily R. and Kivie Kaplan Wing of the Jewish Memorial Hospital

Reception Hall, Boston Dispensary Rehabilitation Institute
Emily R. and Kivie Kaplan Religious Action Center of the
Union of American Hebrew Congregations at Washington,
D.C.

## Affiliations

### CIVIC

Honorary Treasurer, Jewish Memorial Hospital
Director for Life, Jewish Memorial Hospital
Past Chairman, Endowment Fund Committee, Jewish Memorial
Hospital
Treasurer, B'nai B'rith Career and Counseling Services National
Commission
Past Treasurer, Roxbury Cemetery Association
Past President, 210 Associates, Inc.

### RELIGIOUS

Honorary Vice-Chairman, Union of American Hebrew Congrega-
tions
Member, Commission on Social Action of Reform Judaism
Member, Executive Committee and Board of Trustees, Union of
American Hebrew Congregations
Co-founder and Life Trustee, Temple Emanuel, Newton, Mass.
Trustee, Temple Israel, Boston, Mass.

### CULTURAL AND PHILANTHROPIC

Board of Directors, Hebrew Free Loan Society
Life Trustee, Combined Jewish Philanthropies
Past Treasurer and Assistant Treasurer, Combined Jewish Ap-
peal
Life Member of the Board, Brandeis University Associates
Fellow of Brandeis University
Trustee, Emily R. and Kivie Kaplan Family Charitable Trust
Past Member, National Health Planning Committee Council of
Jewish Federations and Welfare Funds

## Awards and Honors

Man of Vision Award, Bonds for Israel Committee
Human Rights Award, NAACP, Pittsburgh, Pa.
Modern Community Developers' First Annual Averell Harriman
   Equal Housing Opportunity Award
Temple Reyim Brotherhood Man-of-the-Year Award
Recipient of T. Kenyon Holly Award for Outstanding Humani-
   tarian Service in Civic, Cultural, and Philanthropic Fields
Honorary Degree, Doctor of Humane Letters, Hebrew Union
   College–Jewish Institute of Religion
Brotherhood Award, Temple Israel, Boston, Mass.
Brotherhood Award, Temple Emanuel, Newton, Mass.

When I asked him for the listing, Kivie sent it to me
reluctantly, with this note appended:

We should remember that the prophet Malachi once asked:
"Have we not all one Father? Hath not one God created us?"

Not only the prophets but our rabbis, and now the experts
in human relations teach us that we strengthen Jews and Judaism
by helping God's children of every faith and every race.

Try to get your friends to understand that, by joining in
fighting bigotry and prejudice, they are also serving Jews and
Judaism by strengthening democracy, furthering brotherhood, and
enhancing human dignity. Tell them to become life members of
the National Association for the Advancement of Colored People
and ask them to remember that discrimination against the Negro
goes hand in hand with discrimination against the Jew.

Yours for justice and peace,
Kivie Kaplan

## Hyperbole and Exaggeration

When we admire and love someone as much as the editors
admire and love Kivie Kaplan it is quite possible inad-
vertently to yield to hyperbole and exaggeration in describing

his character and contributions. We believe that the ensuing chapters written by others attest to the validity of our conviction that Kivie deservedly became a legend in his own time.

As an indication of the esteem in which Kivie was held by the NAACP, the program of the sixty-fifth annual convention, seventeenth annual life membership luncheon, July 3, 1974, in New Orleans, Louisiana, stated the following:

Notwithstanding the numerous other activities of Kivie Kaplan, national president of the NAACP, it can be truly said, he is the architect of the NAACP's life membership program.

This program accounts for as much as three-quarters of a million dollars annually for the national program of the association, as well as supporting the programs of many NAACP branches throughout the nation. As early as 1950, Kivie saw the vast potential of life memberships to underwrite the work of the NAACP.

In 1953, with only 300 life members on the roster, the NAACP National Board of Directors elected Kivie to be chairman of the National Life Membership Committee and he immediately announced a goal of 1,000 life members and later increased the goal to 5,000 and then to 25,000 and finally to 100,000. More than half of his goal has been achieved.

In 1957, the NAACP established the annual Kivie Kaplan Life Membership Awards that would be available to those NAACP branches that made outstanding contributions to the Life Membership Program each year. These awards are presented annually at the life membership luncheon during the national NAACP conventions.

Today, there are sixty life members in the Kaplan family, spanning four generations; fifty-nine are fully paid, the 59th life member in the Kaplan family, Joshua Adam Narva, the first great-grandson of Kivie and his wife Emily, was born on March 17, 1974, in Boston, Massachusetts.

Following the example of previous years, whenever a grandchild or a child is born, Kivie immediately sends a check for $500.00 to cover the full cost of his/her life membership. Without a doubt there are more life members in the Kaplan family than in any other family in the nation or abroad.

Many of the life members who reside in foreign countries were secured by Kivie during his travels abroad.

Almost every week the national office received checks from Kivie covering the cost of life memberships that he had sold. Wherever Kivie went—north, south, east, west or abroad—he sold life memberships.

He took out his personal life membership in 1946. The life memberships that he had sold number in the thousands. However, his most important contribution had been the constant encouragement given to NAACP branch leaders to organize effective and meaningful programs in their efforts to increase life memberships in their communities.

Following the meetings of the Central Conference of American Rabbis in June of 1973, Rabbi Joseph B. Glaser, executive vice-president, sent to Kivie and Emily a copy of the resolution that was voted unanimously.

Rabbi Glaser wrote: "To my knowledge, this is the first time in the eighty-four-year history of the Central Conference that such action is being taken with a resolution. This unique gesture attests to the high esteem in which you are held by the conference." And the resolution stated:

The Central Conference of American Rabbis, meeting in Atlanta — in the heart of the deep south — seeing about it some of the fruits of hard won integration, returning from paying tribute to Martin Luther King, Jr., reaffirms its longstanding commitment to the cause of racial equality and full justice for all people.

This setting called to mind those members of our movement who have stood next to rabbis in the forefront of this struggle.

We pay particular tribute to Kivie Kaplan, president of the NAACP, vice-chairman of the Board of our Union of American Hebrew Congregations, and to Emily Kaplan, patrons of our Religious Action Center in Washington, D.C., and friends of so many of our members. We take pride in them and we are inspired by them.

We pray for them — long and healthy life and sustained involvement in their life work. May they continue to bring credit to our movement and to the house of Israel. And may they see their dream for mankind fulfilled — *bimherah beyamenu* [speedily in our days].

Again the paradox and the paradigm. A conference of rabbis voting a resolution of unanimous tribute to a layman.

## To See the Face of Your Brother

Our age is still grappling and struggling with the question of the ancient psalmist who asked: "What is man?" If we concur with B. F. Skinner and his conviction that we should go beyond freedom and dignity in order to condition and control man to function in a behaviorally proper manner, and if we believe that man is totally conditioned by his environment, controlled by his genes, manipulated by his libido, and determined by the chemical elements on a valence chart, then the example of the life and service of a Kivie Kaplan is irrelevant. If, however, we accept the theological postulate of the Jewish tradition that man assailed by the forces of good and evil is more than a machine, a robot, puppet, computer, or automaton with flesh and blood, then the example of the life and service of Kivie Kaplan is extremely important and relevant to us, to our generation, and to the generations that are yet to be.

That is why this volume is more than a tribute to a man. It is an affirmation of a conviction that every individual is endowed with dignity, sanctity, and the freedom of will to combat evil, to effect the good, and to change himself and his society by translating his faith into the language of action.

Typifying the eternal optimism of the Jewish faith, a faith that refuses to accept defeat or a philosophy of pessimism, a faith that repudiates any ideology of despair, Kivie was an optimist embodying the characteristics of what the prophets called "a prisoner of hope." He refused ever to countenance despair or defeatism. He recognized that progress will be slow, that the advance toward a more universal social justice will be hazardous, difficult, tortuous, and maddeningly faltering, but he stubbornly adhered to his firm belief that the advance *will* be made and tomorrow will witness, if not the realization, then at least the first portents of the fulfillment of the dreams of the prophets and the consecrated ideals of the sages of Israel.

This suggests by way of summary and conclusion a homily from the Jewish tradition that tells of three rabbis who were debating the question: "How do we know when the night ends and the day begins?"

The first rabbi said: "The night ends and a new day begins when you can tell the difference between a blue thread and a purple thread." The second rabbi said: "No, you're wrong. We'll know when it's morning, we'll know when it's light, we'll know when it's a new dawn when we're able to distinguish between a wolf and a dog." The third rabbi disagreed, saying: "You will know when the night ends and the day begins; you will know when there's the coming of the dawn and a new tomorrow, when you can see the face of your brother."

Those who were close to Kivie will always know that he referred to strangers as "brother" or "sister." Day and night he always looked upon the face of a brother or sister. It didn't make any difference whether that face was white, black, or brown. It didn't make any difference whether that face represented one who was a Christian, Muslim, Jew, heretic, atheist, or agnostic. Kivie looked upon the face of every man and woman as the face of his brother and sister. It was a Kivie Kaplan who could enhance our faith and strengthen the conviction that the night can end and through our collective will, and by entering into copartnership with divinity, there can be intimations of a new light, a new dawn, and a new tomorrow of justice, brotherhood, and peace for all humanity.

Here was the man who is now a legend. A legend may be defined as any story coming down from the past, not entirely verifiable. On the other hand, a legend is a story of a life as of a saint or a collection of such stories. Kivie Kaplan was not a saint, but if a legend is a story or collection of stories about the life of a rare, unique, and unusual human being who exemplified priest and prophet, secularist and religionist, particularist and universalist, then Kivie Kaplan was a legend in his own time.

# 2

# The Kaplan Heritage

*Harold J. Berman*

\*

THEY CAME from the *shtetls*—the little Jewish villages of Poland, the Ukraine, Lithuania, and other parts of the Russian Empire — in the last decades of the nineteenth and the first decades of the twentieth centuries, literally by the hundreds of thousands and millions. They were a strange, strange people, something like the Amish of Pennsylvania or the Dukhobors of Canada in their religious fanaticism but with a tremendous respect for learning and for wealth. Not that many of them had much wealth in the old country. And what they had of wealth, like what they had of learning, was supposed to be shared with those who needed it.

Kivie Kaplan's grandparents, on both sides, came from the Kovno (Kaunas) region of Lithuania. His father's father, Rabbi Chaim Elia Kaplan, was a man of great learning and wisdom and great warmth of personality. His mother's grandfather, for whom he was named, was a famous rabbi, Rabbi Akiva.

The children and grandchildren of Chaim Elia Kaplan were all deeply and permanently impressed with the stamp of his character and his spirit. He was born about 1845 (nobody kept very close track of dates). His family had come to Lithuania from "deep Russia." His mother, whose name was Nechama, was called Nechama Tanach ("Nechama the Bible") because of her mastery of the Bible. Chaim Elia would tell his children later that as a boy he had to hide in the rafters to read history books and other secular literature. When he finished the Hebrew grammar school (*cheder*) in the *shtetl*, he was sent, because of his outstanding scholarly ability, to the yeshivah in another town. There, as was the custom, his room and board were furnished by the local families — each week by seven different families. On finishing the course, he was examined by learned rabbis and received the diploma for the rabbinate (*smichah*) with high encomium.

HAROLD BERMAN *is Story Professor of Law at Harvard University. Professor Berman's mother and Kivie Kaplan's father were sister and brother.*

Since learning brought status, Chaim Elia was sought out for marriage by the well-to-do fathers of eligible daughters. His parents arranged his betrothal at the age of thirteen to Chaya Sara Yaffe. Her dowry included a small business and a large house that was used as an inn. The bride helped to manage the inn while the groom went back to his studies. Her parents agreed to support him as a student for five more years, according to the custom called *kest* which was practiced among families that could aspire to marry off a daughter to a "yeshivah boy." Actually, Chaim Elia returned to his bride after only three years.

In 1881 the tsar enacted severely restrictive laws against Jews in the Russian Empire. Chaim Elia Kaplan and his wife Chaya Sara began to think of escape from oppression. Their oldest son, Benjamin, at the age of sixteen, was the first to go to America — to escape conscription for twenty years in the Russian army. Two years later, in 1890, Chaim Elia followed, and shortly thereafter he called for his second son, Morris, aged twelve. Chaim Elia first had a position as a rabbi in Worcester, Massachusetts, but his wife refused to join him there. She did not want to be a "rabbi's wife." He also was glad to give up the formal rabbinate since he did not like to be under the control of unlearned trustees, and his religious interests were primarily scholarly, not priestly or pastoral. He therefore went into the matzah business in Boston, and in 1892 Chaya Sara brought their six young daughters to be with their father and their two brothers.

Almost a century later, it is hard to understand what it meant to be a learned man in the Jewish community, whether in the *shtetl* or in the New World. Learning meant immersion in the Bible, in the commentaries on the Bible called the Talmud, and in the whole literature of Hebrew wisdom that was built around the Bible and the Talmud. It meant endless reading and endless talk with people who came from all over to consult the great man.

As the authors of *Life Is with People* point out:

Learning gives prestige, respect, authority, and status. In the synagogue, the men who sit along the eastern wall, the *mizrach*, are preeminently the learned, and the rabbi, as the most learned of all, has the most honored seat of all—next to the Ark where the Torah is kept. These men are sometimes referred to as "the *mizrach*," sometimes as "the faces," *peney*, of the community. Those at the rear, near the western wall, are the most ignorant. Conversely, it is the unlearned who throng the market place— the women and the untutored workers. If a learned man appears, he walks among the stalls like a visitor from another land and is greeted with deference by those he meets there. He passes by, hardly aware of the piled-up merchandise over which they haggle, for he inhabits a world of the mind. . . . The men who sit along the eastern wall and who live aloof from the market place . . . may be called the *fineh yidn*, the fine Jew; the *eydeleh*, the noble; the *erlicheh*, the honest and pious, . . . *sheyneh liteh*, the beautiful people.*

In the yeshivah, Chaim Elia Kaplan had become accustomed to rising at daybreak and sitting over books until long past midnight. In his middle life, as well, he never slept more than a few hours a night, even when most of his waking hours were spent in the manufacture and sale of matzahs. All his life he always had a book in his hand. The rabbis in Boston and others from as far as Pittsburgh, Cincinnati, and Chicago would come to him for information and advice and wisdom. He would invite them home and they would sleep overnight in his house; if necessary, one of the children would be sent to sleep out in order to make room for the visitor.

Rabbi Kaplan had a great influence on all who came in contact with him, including his young grandson Kivie, who felt particularly close to him. In his religious philosophy he was neither a strict legalist (*misnagid*) nor a mystic (*chasid*), but, in the Lithuanian Jewish tradition, he tried to find the truth in both sides. He was noted for his tolerance and gentle-

* Mark Zborowski and Elizabeth Herzog, *Life Is with People: The Culture of the Shtetl* (New York: Schocken, 1962 [originally published 1952]), p. 73.

ness. His children say that they never in their lives heard him speak ill of anyone. He never scolded his children. Although he enjoyed sitting out on the porch of his house in Roxbury on weekdays, he would refrain from doing so on the Sabbath in order not to embarrass those Jews whom he would otherwise have seen getting off the trolley car — instead of walking, as Jewish law requires — to go to the nearby synagogue.

Once when the young Kivie told his grandfather that he was unable to read the prayer book in Hebrew, Rabbi Kaplan replied that he should read it in English translation — advice which seems entirely natural and even banal today but which at the time was a striking departure from the strict letter of the law which others were teaching.

When Chaim Elia's young son Benjamin, Kivie's father, landed in Boston in 1888, he did what tens of thousands of other immigrants did — he put a pack on his back and went peddling through the streets. He peddled used bottles. In time he saved enough money to start a bottle factory, which eventually employed five-hundred people and was worth $100,000. However, by 1913, machines were replacing men and the factory had to be sold at a great loss. In his early forties, Ben started anew in the theater business, where he again made and lost a fortune. Finally, he went into the leather business, establishing tanneries throughout New England. Here he made his third fortune. He might have lost that one, too, but for the fact that in 1924 his three sons — Joseph (aged twenty-seven), Archie (aged twenty-five), and Kivie (aged twenty) — were able to take over the business.

Kivie had had a taste of high school, but he left it to go into business. Though he loved his grandfather, he was more his father's son — a businessman, not a scholar. Yet making money, for all its fascination, was never an end in itself, either for the father or for the three sons. In the last analysis, the money was to be for the community.

Although Kivie's father was not interested in supporting Jewish religious life, he was an ardent supporter of the development of a Jewish national homeland in Palestine, and he gave substantial sums to that cause. Celia Solomont, Kivie's mother, who was herself from a wealthy family, was for thirty years president and treasurer of the Jewish Women's Convalescent Home in Boston. In addition, her house was visited by a steady stream of people who were raising money for various Jewish causes. When her husband would give her extra money for new clothes at Passover time, Celia would quietly distribute it among her "customers."

The extraordinary philanthropic activities of the three Kaplan brothers — Joseph, Archie, and Kivie — must be understood in the first instance as a product of the same Judaism which manifested itself in the learning and wisdom of Chaim Elia Kaplan. In the *shtetl*, to give was a duty; others could and did demand its fulfillment. For a wealthy person not to give generously — indeed, for any person, including even a poor person, not to give to those in greater need than himself — was considered a violation of Judaic law. Here again one can do no better than to quote from *Life Is with People*. The word for charity in the *shtetl*, the authors point out, is *tsedakah*, which means not compassion but righteousness — justice.

Life in the *shtetl* begins and ends with *tsedakah*. When a child is born, the father pledges a certain amount of money for distribution to the poor. At a funeral the mourners distribute coins to the beggars who swarm the cemetery, chanting "*Tsedakah* will save from death." At every turn during one's life, the reminder to give is present. At the circumcision ceremony, the boy consecrated to the Covenant is specifically dedicated to good deeds. Every celebration, every holiday is accompanied by gifts to the needy. . . .

On earth, the prestige value of good deeds is second only to that of learning. . . . The man who is known as a great benefactor receives honorific deference, *koved*. . . . For the "love of *koved*" one will pour out his substance in charitable activities. . . . The one who gives greatly is called *baal tsedakah*, master of charity, one of the most honored titles a man can win. The master of charity is one who contributes largely to community services, gives alms to beggars, always has a . . . stranger-guest for the Sabbath or holiday meals, is ready to give a loan when his neighbor is short of money. . . . A pauper, a poor relative, is always welcomed and never leaves "with empty hands." Moreover, the real master of charity gives much that is known only to him and to God.*

This continual display of righteousness gives a man prestige, status, merit — almost, though not quite, to the same extent as learning. As Zborowski and Herzog indicate, the "simple" man, the "common" man, is one who is neither learned nor giving; the "fine" man, the "beautiful" man, is either learned (in which case he will surely give money if he has it, since his learning is at the same time wisdom and morality) or, if he is not learned, at least philanthropic.

The other side of the coin — security, power, vanity — is not rejected or even disparaged, but it is not expressly valued: it does not lead to honor or to merit.

Thus the family background of a man like Kivie Kaplan tells us a great deal about his character and personality. The connections between the traditional Jewish conception of tsedakah, righteousness, the social duty to give, the social privilege of giving, on the one hand, and the particular Kivie Kaplan brand of philanthropy, on the other, were obvious to anyone who watched him in action. He would tell someone, for example, that he was about to do him a very great favor — namely, allow him to buy a life membership in the NAACP.

Yet in Kivie Kaplan something was added — by America — to traditional Jewish concepts of social justice, something which went beyond the dimensions of the shtetl. The community has been widened to include other races and other religions. Thereby both righteousness and compassion were expanded in new directions. Loyalty to one's people was combined with a keener sense of the oneness of humankind. This may have been more than his grandparents bargained for when they left the shtetl and crossed the sea in ships to start a new life in the New World; but Chaim Elia, at least, would have understood and would have given his blessing, and for Kivie that was important.

* Zborowski and Herzog, Life Is with People, pp. 193, 195–96.

# 3

## The Family Man

### Edward K. Kaplan

*

MEMORIES pass through filters along the way to consciousness, and facts grow quickly into interpretations. Asked to write a slice of intimate history, especially that of a "legendary" father, a son must attempt strong efforts to be objective. The picture which emerges from this pen is far from complete, necessarily, for love often tempers the historian's scientific eye. Proust's dilemma put back to shelf, I accept the challenge of the Baal Shem Tov, the founder of Chasidism: to seek the sparks of holiness in the daily turmoil. What follows, then, is not history in its rigorous sense, but an attempt to grasp — through memories — some basic patterns of a life and personality which define Kivie Kaplan as a family man.

In this task I have been aided by my parents, my mother's sisters, Aunts Frances Glaser and Elizabeth Tavel, my two sisters, Sylvia Grossman and Jean Green; by my wife and friend Sandy, who shared my thoughts and uncertainties with a love nourished with professional acumen; and Robert May, whose companionship on this journey has been significantly felt and appreciated. The friendship of Dr. Howard Thurman has also nourished my perspective in a fundamental way. Yet I take responsibility for what is certainly an inadequate portrait. To my sisters Jean and Sylvia, who have always shown me a deep and understanding love, I dedicate these few pages of a family album.

Kivie found his lifelong companion at about the age of twelve, and apparently decided at that time that he wanted to marry her. Emily Rogers was the second oldest daughter in a family of four girls and four boys who lived in a large old house in Chelsea, Massachusetts. Kivie (a third cousin) would visit Emily, always bringing some sort of candy and goodies, which the little sisters would sometimes snitch from her bureau drawers. Kivie was extremely shy and would blush to the roots when someone would walk into the room,

EDWARD KAPLAN *is assistant professor of French and religion at Amherst College.*

though he was always innocent of indiscretion. His gifts to Emily's brothers and sisters must have been a way for him to break the ice, extend himself outward, and to overcome a timidity in conversations over which he did not have full control. As he grew older, Kivie called on Emily in one of the first Fords in the neighborhood. Emily was a beautiful, dark-haired, and frail young woman who had many admirers. Kivie seems to have won her through persistence and faithful dedication, traits which marked him in all his endeavors. They were married on June 3, 1925, at the Beacon House in Brookline. Kivie was twenty-one and Emily was twenty.

I would venture to say that my father never looked at another woman after falling in love with Emily. He never had an interest in women even as objects of beauty — a hypothesis I tested unwittingly with girlfriends I would bring home for family inspection. (They never passed.) Dad's dedication to mother was an example of incredible purity of intention. During her senior year at Girls' Latin School, Emily had a bout with Saint Vitus' dance (chorea), and because of her delicate nerves Kivie promised her mother that Emily would never have to work hard and that he would always take special care of her. This remained one of the main aims of his hus-bandship, and we always had help who looked after the chil-dren and did the cooking, because mother was often sick and weak. Their marriage was a traditional one, typical of most of the generations preceding our own: the wife would sacrifice her potential autonomy to the career and social support of the husband, while he, realizing the value of this arrangement, would worship and protect the wife. Emily had been an out-standing student in high school (her straight A's in French always encouraged me in that realm), and, although she had been accepted at Wellesley College (where her sister Eliza-beth had gone), she did not go to college, preferring to link her destinies to those of the young businessman of twenty-one. There is always a special warmth about mother, who under-stands better than father did the inner life of feelings, though both rarely talked about the other directly. Her beauty and social charm helped Dad through his years of reaching outward into the community.

Dad was never much of a student in high school. He went to English High and reported to me that the activity he enjoyed most was math class, for he made friends with the teacher so that he could go out and eat ice cream; he also enjoyed working with numbers (but not the kind I would bring home from my math classes). Young Kivie also became treasurer of some neighborhood kids' group, starting another life pattern. With some pride and humor, he said that the only way he could graduate from high school was to join the glee club. By age thirteen Kivie was working for his father, Benjamin Kaplan, in the various businesses that he tried and thus learned the value of hard work and self-discipline. It is difficult for me to discern the influence of Grandpa Kaplan on Dad, since I was very young when he died and have to rely on scant memories. By all accounts, he was an erratic businessman, earning and losing several fortunes. He seemed to have been a stubborn and tough person and paid his boys poorly. Because Kivie was the youngest, he was the "apple of his father's eye." Dad would not tell me if his father was the apple of his. Kivie said that he learned many negative lessons from his father about becoming a successful businessman, the goal of his early life.

Another situation I know little about concerns the fact that Benjamin Kaplan was, for the latter years of his life, separated from his wife Celia. Those kinds of things were never mentioned in our family, and it is only now that I found out. His was a generation that hid sadness and pain. But I suspect that this fact might have contributed significantly to my father's strong fidelity to the concept of family. Kivie had a veritable religion of family, always seeking to group them around him, and, despite the remarkable differences between us, persisting in hoping that the families of his three children would find their greatest joys together. Kivie himself considered his duty as a son to be paramount, and, after the death of Grandpa Kaplan, Grandmother Celia was a frequent visitor at our family dinners. Tensions within the family were less significant to Kivie than the hope of harmony.

But to return to Kivie and Emily at the beginning: by the time they were married, the three Kaplan brothers — Joe, Archie, and Kivie — had started the Colonial Tanning Company. They did most of the work themselves, and Dad reported that he used to work twelve to eighteen hours a day; sometimes even the wives came in and helped pack, sort, and ship the leather. To combine business with holidays, Kivie was given the assignment to sell a quantity of leather on his honeymoon. So he set off with his new bride and some cases of leather. Miracle of miracles, he sold it all even before the end of the crossing. This was a first example of Kivie's remarkable salesman's ability, a talent which he would use both to earn money and to draw it from others in his various charitable endeavors. The honeymooners spent the rest of their conjugal journey in Central America, with special affection for Cuba and Haiti. Always staying with a successful pattern, Kivie traveled almost exclusively to these countries and others in Central America before he discovered Europe in the 1950s. Thus another pattern developed: sales trips to countries which were also vacation spots. Kivie tried not to separate pleasure from the serious task of selling.

One year and nine months after their marriage the first daughter, Sylvia, was born on March 12, 1927. At that time they moved from Bowdoin Street in Dorchester to a two-family house on Claybourne Street in the same town. When Jean was born three years later (July 29, 1930), they moved to a small brick house on Rowena Road in Newton; and when twelve years later the present writer was born (March 4, 1942), we all moved to a large white brick house, obviously the dwelling of a more prosperous man, on Hammond Street in Chestnut Hill. This is where many of the readers of the present volume may remember visiting, for here is where Kivie really

opened to the world. In 1969, after the children had settled down in their own worlds, our parents moved to a luxury
apartment on Boylston Street in Chestnut Hill. Living habits
were slightly adjusted but not changed. It is interesting to
note that the families of Sylvia and Jean, not only remained in
Newton, but stayed within easy reach of my parents. This
was certainly an essential part of Kivie's cherished ideal of
family unity.

During the middle years of growing prosperity on Rowena Road, Dad became active in community affairs: he was an
air raid warden, active in the Newton Community Chest, and
had a victory garden on which the girls' various boyfriends
might be called to help work.

During the Rowena Road period, he also developed cus-
toms meant to keep his family in touch with the rest of the
relatives, especially mother's family. Someone called Kivie
"the godfather of the Rogers family," and I think this was
quite correct. My mother's family can be characterized generally as a group of good, gentle, unpretentious people, coming from a poor background, and, after the stock market crash
and the Depression, remaining relatively poor — to the extent
that they would often use our old clothing. Dad helped
finance the education of some of their children. They nevertheless had, each of them, a certain strength and dignity which,
in some ways, outlasts the more obvious accomplishments of
their benefactor.

They remain in my memory as much myths as people,
myths because my father had a nickname for each of them (a
typical way of his relating to people), which helped them
to find their place in the scene reenacted every Sunday afternoon and evening at our house. The memory of this routine
creates a warm feeling in me, although, as I decompose it
into its own separate realities, I often wonder what those
gatherings were about. However, they did contribute to a certain degree to the family cohesiveness which my father valued
above all.

The stars of the show were perhaps the "maiden aunts," Annie and Sarah, whom my father called "the twins" and teased them about nonexistent millionaires from South America waiting to marry them in great splendor. Annie was a fat, bustling, drinking, and heavy-smoking woman, loose in her language and generous with her laughter, outgoing and jovial. I remember watching with her old films on television, and she would cackle and tell me how many of the stars she knew from her newsstand in the Hotel Touraine in Boston. Sarah was more quiet but had many hidden talents; like all the younger Rogers women, she had a sharp intelligence. In her young days she had done some acting and was an executive secretary for some firm. Annie's job, as Dad put it, was to "put big things in little boxes" at a jewelry store. Sarah was not as boisterous as Annie, but they both made those Sundays something to look forward to.

There was also "Uncle Ed Long who happened to be short" (I give the nicknames invented by Dad in quotation marks), a jolly person who imitated Charlie Chaplin and who always tried to give a special joy to people wherever he was. His wife, Eunice, "Little Eutzke," was overweight and quiet; but, when she ventured a word, her wit shone with cleverness and good sense. Uncle Ben Tavel, "Bendid Buruch," was another highlight. Uncle Ben smoked big cigars and liked to drink and play the horses. I think it took him over thirty years to get my father to abandon his puritanical disrespect of the horses and accompany him and Aunt Bessie to the track. (By the way, Dad never smoked in his life and started drinking only in his later years. Beefeater gin — only — lots of ice, Schweppes tonic, with two limes — nothing else.) Ben's wife Bessie, a Wellesley graduate, a clearheaded and sensible person, was a very supportive wife and mother and independent in her opinions. Also present would be Uncle Rob (mother's brother) and Aunt Frances, "Miss Ginsberg," whom my father ribbed without mercy. Aunt Frances was the aristocrat of the family, at least in manners, conservative in her speech and taste, and overbearing on sweet

Uncle Rob, meek and mild, who took it like a lamb. Kivie many a time had his revenge on "Miss Ginsberg," who never lost her cool, kidding her about black people and various liberal causes in which Dad could never get her interested.

Here is the scene. Kivie sits in his favorite chair, in a strategic corner of the room. Mother's relatives sit around. The family talk flows and evaporates, and mother shuffles around serving fruit and candy. Kivie might have been fairly quiet at first, but, as his outside activities increased and he met more and more interesting people and received more and more awards, he would hold court and tell us all about his adventures. At dinner time, we go to the breakfast room, drink borscht, and eat bagels and lox. On those Sundays, no help, no formal service; just fellowship and family. Those enjoyable visits continued for many years.

Another custom which defined the family for us was the Friday night dinner, Shabbat dinner. I understand that these started at my Grandmother Rogers's house, and when she became too sick and finally died they were held at our house. I remember the ones held at Hammond Street, which many of the present readers might have attended. (You notice that much of our visiting with people revolved around eating, which was more than just nourishment — it was a way of relating.) Dad would say *Kiddush*, mother would light the candles, and Mrs. Georgiana Dotson—a wonderful woman who worked for us with her husband Charles for about thirteen years and in large part brought me up — would bring in the roast beef. I think that even then mother criticized Dad's carving of it. Sylvia and Jean, then their husbands and growing families, would attend, and of course Grandmother Kaplan, Celia (a little more about her soon). "Little Edward," as I was in the old days, started out in the room with the grownups, but often my behavior was bad and, when I made one false move too many, I was sent, sometimes dragged by force, into the kitchen to finish my meal with Georgiana and Charles. (When I look back on this, it is with fondness, strangely enough.)

Sylvia met and married Morton Grossman, whom Dad

called "Timber" (because he was in the lumber business),
and, when Jean married Al Green soon after, he also became
part of our family. Al Green, a podiatrist, soon became "Dr.
Green, I believe" and later "Ref" (meaning "Reverend Green,"
because of his traditional religious observances). These dinners continued long after the family really got too large to
handle — we even tried having it in a restaurant or a special
room in a country club — but then we had to give it up. They
always remained an ideal image for my father, who always
attempted to get the entire family, including grandchildren
and their spouses, together at one time in a single place.

Grandmother Kaplan was an important feature of these
dinners, and she would come to dinner at our house several times during the week. During the time I knew her, she
had hardening of the arteries and was very depressed. She
would arrive before dinner and sit in a corner and moan and
groan, in a singsong manner. "Oy, oy, oy. . ." she would
sing. Little imp that I was, I tried to entertain her, make her
tell her favorite stories that would cause her to chuckle. As a
result I gained her homage and support when I acted up at the
table, and she would say, "Well, Edward is a fine little man."
She was right, of course, but grandmother's logic did not
make the table more peaceful, so back to the kitchen I went.
The great lesson I learned from the way Dad took care of
grandmother was one of devotion to the downtrodden and
lonely. In her active days, Celia Kaplan was president and
treasurer of the Jewish Women's Convalescent Home for
over thirty years, a woman of great poise, dignity, and compassion. By the time of which I speak, Grandma was not
really a lot of fun, yet Kivie remained completely faithful to
her. She was a wise and sweet person who had taught him the
value of charity, and he never forgot that lesson. It was an
obscure but important privilege for us to spend that time with
her in our house.

It was interesting to see how Dad connected his faithful-
ness to the family with his bringing up of children. Sylvia and

Jean were, of course, taken often to various special places in Boston: the Franklin Park Zoo, the Aquarium, the Children's Museum, the swanboats at Boston Public Gardens, Plymouth Rock. But they would also be taken to visit various older members of the family on Sunday mornings. Jean remembers in particular visits to "Marsha de berya" (the great housewife), Grandfather Kaplan's sister, who would serve delicious cakes to the little girls (hence the nickname). Other visits to Grandpa Ben Kaplan were memorable because he used to drink his tea in a glass, holding a cube of sugar between his teeth. Visits were also made to Rabbi and Rebbetzin Mostovski, especially to enjoy their *sukah*. The grandchildren would also visit those of the elders who remained. Kivie really respected and enjoyed these old people, and he wanted to share the joy of his young family with them. Dad always felt a deep responsibility toward the older members of his family. This was one of the other rituals of his religion of family.

Another custom which should be recorded was the annual May 30 weekend trip to North Bridgeton, Maine, with other members of the Rogers family and their children. They would have picnics and other kinds of fun. (It was on one of those trips, I believe, that Dad got a taste of anti-Semitism which would influence his dedication to civil rights in later years.) And each year the extended family would have a Chanukah party, a feast of presents and entertainment by the children and grandchildren, until the crowd got too large for my parents to handle. Also customary was a trip to New York alone with Dad when a child would reach age ten. He would show each of us in our turn "the big city."

Kivie as an individual, though extremely stubborn and independent and enjoying his eccentricity, did let himself be influenced by people he recognized as special, like his mother. As he mentioned in newspaper interviews, she taught him the pleasures of charity and, after her illness, the virtues of devotion to the sick. Other family influences must have pushed Dad in certain directions of self-assertion and individuality. If one is truly interested in understanding the personality of my father, he would do well to explore his relationship with his two brothers, Joe and Archie. He had no sisters. Starting the family business together, they remained together, both professionally and socially, for many years; and then, through the vicissitudes of their separate needs and personalities, personal competition, and business problems, they eventually broke up.

The oldest of the brothers, Joe Kaplan, was unofficially the public relations man of the company. He was an extrovert, extremely charming and warm; he loved to travel all over the world and he spoke several languages. He graduated from Boston University, had an electrifying effect on people in social situations because of his extraordinary skill in telling unforgettable stories (many in humorous dialect). Kivie seemed to be somewhat put off by Joe's social ease and was often doubtful of his value as a businessman. Whatever one might say, Joe was always remembered and loved, and his *joie de vivre* might have had something to do with my father's puritanism. Archie was something else. More serious, dour, even grim, very moralistic, he attended MIT and shared Kivie's stubbornness. Very sentimental about the family in his old age (when I met him, after many years, at his grandson's bar mitzvah), he was nevertheless unable to break a silence with my father which lasted about fifteen years — even though they lived on the same street in Newton for thirty years. Archie was also interested in charity, but on a smaller scale, and he never developed the outgoing aggressiveness which made Dad a successful fund raiser and public speaker. Given the stubbornness and self-righteousness characteristic of all the family, I would not venture to guess who was at fault. It was a tragic contrast to the good relations Dad always had with the Rogers family.

But those sad events did not transpire until rather late in a full life. Let us return to the years of Kivie's formative period, to another personal quirk, his preoccupation with health.

Those who knew him for a long time remember that Kivie was a health culturist in the early 1930s. One of his strong habits was to play tennis every morning from seven to eight, early enough so that he could "have more time with the family," as he told me. On Sundays he would play from nine to ten. This continued until my mother's brother Kivey (it is a family name) died of a heart attack on the court (1943). Typical of Kivie's all-or-nothing approach, he gave up tennis entirely and switched to walking. He would often walk to work from Newton to downtown Boston and took his children out on long walks in the woods. I remember walks in the Hammond Pond Park woods with Dad when I was a boy.

But a real turning point in his life came with his discovery of the Bernarr Macfadden Health Spa in Dansville, New York. You may remember old Bernarr Macfadden, the guy who used to parachute out of an airplane every year until he died in his eighties. According to Dad, his Macfadden period had a deep psychological impact on him. It is there, I guess, that he developed his optimistic and rationalistic view of the individual, the view that anyone could solve personal and health problems just by thinking and eating right. The main principle he often quoted is this: "A person who eats right, but doesn't think right, can still be sick," and various combinations of the same. So Kivie tried to follow a rigorous diet of correct food and right thoughts. He borrowed and made his trademark the now-legendary "Keep Smiling" cards, and his clear advice to people followed in a similar vein. All during my stormy adolescence, when I wanted to express anger, for example, he would counter: "The man who keeps cool has the advantage." Or another: "Try to disagree without being disagreeable." This, of course, was excellent advice, but in the context of a family battle it was sometimes disconcertingly ineffective.

It is interesting to see how Kivie developed his optimism. How did Dad get to Macfadden's in the first place? When the Colonial Tanning brothers wanted to take out a large life insurance policy, Kivie was examined medically and pronounced overweight and unfit; so to save the premium money, they sent him to Macfadden's to reduce. There he lost fifty pounds, but it was the start of a pattern of losing a lot of weight quickly and gaining it back. The keynote of this health resort, then, was diet and mental conditioning. Some of my parents' fondest memories are the inspirational songs they would sing at Macfadden's. Here is a sample:

> *Brighten the corner where you are,* [repeat]
> *Make somebody happy,*
> *Sing a song along the way,*
> *Brighten the corner when you may.*

And (to the tune of "Jingle Bells"):

> *Orange juice, orange juice*
> *Drink it every day. . . .*

I hope the reader will forgive me for these meager examples, but, when Dad was telling me about this, he thought of finding the songbooks and — yes — possibly giving them out to people again.

In response to the success of Macfadden's, the three brothers opened up a lunchroom at Colonial Tanning Company, where health foods were served. *All* employees, labor and management, ate in the same room and had the right to free hot lunches. This lunchroom was important for another reason, less concerned with business. A system of "CARE packages" evolved: Irene Glasser, the lady who ran the Colonial lunchroom, would prepare packages of food for Dad to distribute — or, rather, for his children to deliver. For Kivie always followed his executive's motto: Never do yourself what you can get others to do for you. Delivery of packages was part of our "character training." Jean and Sylvia when very young had to take out the garbage and do various jobs around the house; they had to keep a precise log of expenditure of their allowances. And my main task, after I got my driver's license, was to deliver these packages. I remember doing this especially on Martha's Vineyard.

Starting his lifelong habit of giving gifts during this health food period, Dad would order cases — he never did anything in moderation — of dried and exotic fruit, like mangoes, cherimoyas, and Cranshaw melon when they were just being developed. I remember clearly one hot summer evening on our patio, drooling and slurping over mangoes impaled on special forks. Dad also had a machine to make vegetable juices. From this time on he developed a system of distribution — for he would never call on someone without bringing something.

Excessive gifts were his trademark. In addition to goodies, he distributed books — mostly books written by people he knew personally — pamphlets, and all sorts of information about civil rights and the fight for justice, and, from time to time, reproductions of articles about himself, interviews in papers, even hate articles that appeared in right-wing, anti-Semitic, and antiblack papers (like the *New Orleans Thunderbolt*). He was always sharing his abundant life with other people, from the very start of the relationship. That is a segment of the genesis of that particular part of the legend.

As I try to remember the best moments of my growing up with Dad, I think that we were closest when we worked together at Colonial Tanning Company. For some reason, during my teenage years I was becoming difficult to manage and even a bit delinquent. I started to smoke a lot when I was fourteen, despite Dad's constant opposition to smoking, and was unruly in school. Aunt Frances still remembers with horror young Edward flipping his cigarette butts into the family fireplace. I became so bad that my parents, unable to cope, had to do something drastic. Dad consulted Dr. John Cooke, our family dentist and a graduate of Harvard, who suggested prep school. I failed the entrance exam for Andover, and Dr. Cooke, the dentist of the headmaster of Deerfield Academy, got me in there, where I was turned into a "gentleman." The best moments of those dismal three years of exile were when my parents drove up and took me out with some friends for a hearty meal at Wiggins Tavern in Northampton.

My real separation from the family, then, came at about age fifteen when I was sent to Deerfield to become civilized. After that, relations with the family were really rather formally limited to visits and, at the beginning, working with Dad.

Many of my early childhood memories with Kivie converge upon ceremonial functions to honor my father, at which people would inevitably say to me, "You should be very proud of your father," "I hope you will fill your father's shoes," and some such rot, and I had to imagine something decent to say in return. When I worked with him, I was the "boss's son," but a little more. I was in training — according to the time-worn custom of the free enterprise system — to take over my father's managerial place in the company (he was president and general manager by the time we got out of it). This was a time of close companionship with Dad.

One of his business maxims was to be first in the office in the morning and last out at night. So we would drive into town in his Cadillac, leaving the house around 7–7:30 A.M.; along the way he would point out the other fat cats in their big cars, explaining that they were successful because they worked hard. My own job at that time was in the shipping department, and I really enjoyed the company of the workers, who swore, told fascinating stories, goldbricked, and smoked — all good fun for me.

My training at Colonial Tanning I see as typical of my father's role as an educator. He put an expert in charge of me: George Silva, his heavy and witty assistant general manager, who had worked his way up to that post from being a worker in a shoe factory. George was an excellent pedagogue, laconic and sharp, critical and truly interested in what I learned. Kivie was more aphoristic and explained less to me than George did. Dad conceived the general plan of action, which was to put me in the various departments, where the experts would teach me what they knew. While with Dad I often met with customers, who yielded an important entertainment value, since many of them were quite eccentric.

Besides sitting in on these upper-level sessions, I would go on trips with the company's salesmen to learn salesmanship. At the end of a workday I would go home with Dad or with the comptroller "Curly" Goldfarb (another one of Dad's loaded nicknames: Ed Goldfarb was as bald as a billiard ball).

High points were business trips, like the one to the shoe convention in New York with the "boys": Dick Goldberg, who was the only one in the company with a college education and who carried a slide rule (and used it); John Mercon, stone-faced, a stern looking Catholic who had the neatest desk in the office and always had figures at the tip of his tongue; the disorderly and inspired Sam Rubin, with his jutting jaw and hot temper. One evening in New York we went to a Rumanian Jewish restaurant on Second Avenue and Second Street, Moskowitz and Lupowitz, where we ate as much of this exotic cuisine as possible, making more room by drinking bottled seltzer water and burping. Those were the days of excellent comradeship, and my fantasies of being a manager of all this nourished my sense of power and potential. I felt very close to Dad on these trips, when we shared a hotel room, and I saw how a successful businessman operated. He was utterly honest in everything he did; that was impressive, even in those days. Colonial Tanning Company was like a family for him, though he never had anything to do with his co-workers outside the business situation.

An important part of this relationship was my job as "court jester" for Dad. My specialty was imitations of various characters we would meet. This routine continued for many years, until I utterly refused to do any more (say, about age twenty-five, maybe even later), but he continued to meekly ask: "How would Harry say it?" (Poor old Harry had a peculiar voice.) Another area of my "expertise" was to make funny faces. Kivie was easy to delight in this way and was unwilling for me to outgrow this habit before he did.

It was characteristic of Kivie never to let a good joke go: it should be used to its utmost and die a slow natural death.

This portrait of Kivie's humor would be incomplete without mention of our Funny Name Club. Let two examples suffice. (Excuse me for introducing the names of two people that are funny only when detached from their persons.) One was Pincus Medwed, whom I ended up sitting next to at a nephew's bar mitzvah and whom I thank sincerely for an extremely interesting conversation on the Kabbalah. The other was Golden Frinks, a civil rights worker from North Carolina, an outstanding community organizer. To have some fun, Dad called up my sister Jean and told her about meeting Golden Frinks, and she, being quite aware of his habit of "put-ons," refused to believe him. Imagine her surprise upon meeting the excellent Mr. Frinks one evening at his house. Another lovely devilish thing that Kivie did was to have his picture taken with a 350-pound gentleman at an NAACP meeting — to counteract accusations that Kivie was fat. This trophy was hung proudly along with other awards on Kivie's display walls. You can see the delight on the fat man's face at having his picture taken with the president of the NAACP, and you can also glimpse the imperceptible chuckle on the president's controlled lips, enjoying his little trick. Such fun Dad was always willing to have.

A much more significant sharing came when Dad would take me to national conventions of the NAACP. Here he would be in his fullest glory, adulated by the people for his great fundraising accomplishments and for his blunt advice and inspirational salesmanship of life memberships. He was also very interested in the youths who attended those meetings, and it would be our privilege to have meals and conversations with many outstanding young people. On the occasion of the Selma-Montgomery march headed by Dr. Martin Luther King, Jr., he proudly told people that he was accompanied on that march by his son and his grandson Louis Grossman — three generations! The march was a significant event in all our lives. My wife Sandy and I once went with him to the NAACP convention in Jackson, Mississippi. Sharing directly some of Dad's unique experiences related to civil rights was the best way of understanding the pleasures and pains of his mission.

A very crucial moment in both our lives came in 1961, when we were all in Pennsylvania to attend an honorary degree presentation to Dad and Martin Luther King, Jr., at Lincoln University. In our motel room, just before a dinner party given for us by some friends, Dad received a phone call that his tannery in Ayer, Massachusetts, had just burned down. It had been the main means of production of Colonial Tanning. He controlled himself and did not mention any of this to anyone that evening. But soon after, he discussed it with me and asked me if he should rebuild the business for me. He said that the only reason for him to continue in business now was to leave something for me, since he had already made enough money for the security of our immediate family. At that moment, he let me decide the course of his life and mine, and we opted for a potential liquidation of the business since I was thinking seriously of getting into college teaching. He was detached enough from his identity as a businessman and sufficiently respected my own desires and independence to give me that choice. (Dad's version of that incident is somewhat different: He felt that, because he was not so completely involved in business life, he wanted to give it up before I made my vocational commitment. It may be true. Let the ambiguity remain, for they both are constructions of the self-image of the beholder.)

All his adult life, Kivie was interested in service to the community. Because of personal experiences of anti-Semitism and prejudice against blacks, he became involved in the NAACP at the local level. But it was not until he met Professor S. Ralph Harlow, a teacher of religion at Smith College for thirty years, Congregational minister and radical political activist, that he worked on a national scale. It was Ralph who convinced the national board of the NAACP to take on Kivie Kaplan who then became instrumental in much of their financial success.

But Ralph Harlow's influence was even more fundamental

to my father, for Ralph gave all of us a deepened vision of reality and accompanied Dad throughout his moral career. They met around 1938, in connection with the marriage of Kivie's first cousin, Harold J. Berman, to Ralph's daughter, Ruth. In this situation another one of Kivie's characteristic traits was evident. Hal Berman had converted to Christianity before he met Ruth, and he had great difficulties with his Jewish family in this regard. Dad supported Harold in every way possible, pointing out the slackness of his family's Jewish observance. The strength of Kivie's support for Hal, I am sure, had an effect upon reconciling his family with him. Kivie was always the champion of the convert and was even tolerant of mixed marriages. He had a basic respect for the integrity of religious observances and could spot hypocrisy and moral inconsistency when he saw it.

When Dad first met Ralph Harlow, it was, to use his own words, "love at first sight." (Dad often used certain idioms without realizing exactly what they can connote.) Through this friendship Dad strengthened and broadened his interest in social justice for all peoples, for Ralph was a professor as well as a religious Christian, and he was one of the founders of the American Christian Palestine Committee. In fact, Dad used to accompany Ralph on many of his debates with Arab opponents of Palestine for the Jews. Ralph's great learning in religion and philosophy, his special love for the Hebrew prophets, brought to Dad a clearer formulation of what he himself was about. Ralph's and his wife Marion's radicalism often pleased Dad, who, though he was not afraid of using money, had a fundamental respect for those who did not value it. Here is how Ralph, in a letter to Kivie dated April 4, 1962, described the basic difference between their two approaches to the social action struggle:

*Dear Kivie:*
I have been lying on my couch thinking of a letter to write you. It would take over 20 pages at the least, and you have no time and neither do I at the present, to include all I want to say. . . .

Briefly, what I mean by your "feeling deeply but seeing dimly" is this. Your field has been business, not philosophy, certainly not theology, as mine has been. Back of our fight for justice is an *ideal*, spoken by the prophets, seers and poets of *all* races and nations. "God hath not left Himself without a witness anywhere," as the Scripture says.

Many people know the prophetic message, are well versed in the philosophy and theology, but LACK the emotional response, and our minds will never take us an inch that our hearts do not respond to. You have done little reading and study in the philosophy and ideas that lie back of this struggle for justice, but you deeply FEEL it. Take a few examples; the ten commandments were in the Code of Hammurabi, a thousand years before Moses lived. But the concept of ONE GOD, a God of justice, flamed in the message of the Hebrew prophets.

. . . [There] are people who see, who know the intellectual truth of the way they deny in life, because they lack the emotion that a Martin Luther King, an Isaiah, a Micah *felt*. YOU HAVE THE EMOTION.

The trouble with religion, patriotism, even family loyalty is that the IDEAL on which they are founded and that inspired them has been LOST in ideology, in rituals, in kitchens, in hundreds of "laws" and traditions the FOUNDERS never knew and which the prophets of the IDEAL have attacked as the real enemies of true religion and patriotism. Read Isaiah 1: 10–18. Jeremiah 31: 31–34. St. John 4: 19–24. . . .

My love to you and Emily

[Signed] Ralph.


Ralph was one of the few people Dad knew and respected enough to accept criticism and advice from. In fact, Dad, who had little time to read and had not developed the habit, asked Ralph to supervise his education. Ralph would give him a list of books that he had read and found worthwhile, and Kivie would read what he could. Kivie must have started a number of books in this way, but it wasn't until his retirement from business in 1963 that he really read a number of books from cover to cover. And he gave them away like candy, many of them read by him — written by friends of his or concerning the social justice struggle, and he tried his best to have them autographed by the author. When asked to describe the contents of what he read, his communication was usually concise: "a blockbuster," "terrific," "really tells it like it is." Dad was a man of few words and many actions.

After I was born in 1942, my parents changed their habit of spending the summers in Maine and found Martha's Vineyard where they would rent a house every summer. They never let a good thing go. The Harlows also had a house on the Vineyard, which Ralph had inherited from his own father, and a wonderful community was formed at the "Lagoon" — a group of ministers, rabbis, professors, all liberal and natural people. Every Sunday night there would be a sing at the house of Marion and Ralph, which made a tremendous impression on me. I remember Dad's reaction when some of the Jewish guests objected to the singing of hymns that contained the word "Jesus." This did not bother Dad, and he always felt that we should be more liberal when fellowship was concerned. Dad shared Ralph's friendship with me, and, because of Ralph's direct and persistent advice and my father's willingness to let me decide for myself, I rejected the path of businessman for the vocation of teacher and scholar. Much of Ralph penetrated both my father and myself. I believe that Ralph always remained a father for all of us.

A good example of how differently Ralph and Kivie approached personal problems concerns advice given to me on sexual morality. Just before I went to France for my junior year of college, Dad had a serious talk with me, the gist of which was his wish for me to remain a virgin before marriage. You know, Paris is the city where women fall all over themselves to sleep with a man — we both imagined. (*Pas vrai.*) Dad gave me the usual talk about VD, women conniving to marry you, and the like. I fought his wish for me to make an official promise about my virginity, and finally he agreed to have it arbitrated by Ralph Harlow. Dad was always willing to admit special expertise in other people, and Ralph qualified in the domain of morals. Ralph gave me the best advice on sexual relations that I have ever heard: "Eddie," he said, "never sleep with a girl you do not want to be the mother of your child." That took the dilemma out of the context of puritanical principles and into that of interpersonal relations. Dad was open-minded enough to surrender his authority to Ralph, though he did not change his mind or understand what Ralph meant.

Let us see the more successful side of Kivie's dedication to a clear-cut moral life. Because of Ralph and his friends, and Dad's association with the UAHC and the NAACP, Dad also got to know many clergymen. It soon became a common experience to have dinner with many of them. It must have been hard for Dad to host so many rabbis, ministers, priests, and professors. He always sadly remarked to mother when she criticized his bad grammar, "You didn't marry a college professor" — and later added "but you bore one" (that is, gave birth to one). Kivie respected and admired these educated people, because they shared one sublime value with him: the dedication to justice and peace for all people. Some of these people were intellectuals, but they were all activists, the kind of people my father could understand. And they all admired him. These companions also watered my roots, as they did my father's.

How difficult it must have been for him to compare his education to theirs — but only for a moment. For he received so many long and beautifully written letters full of clerical eloquence, recognizing him as a senior partner in a common cause. As his own moral career advanced, Kivie began to be recognized by the academic world, receiving many honorary degrees. He had a love for all kinds of people and believed in the natural superiority of the poor who were rich in spirit, the living flame of the social conscience which he shared with so many. He saw dimly but felt deeply. And he touched numerous lives because of his overweening dedication to justice.

If there was shining gold to be drawn from this active life, the family of Kivie also collected some dross, an alloy of otherness. Some of my earliest childhood memories (the ones that usually come up on the couch) are of holding my father's hand at some function in honor of him and playing the role of a passive and faithful son. This is all to warn the reader that what follows may be less objective than it should be — or perhaps too objective.

Kivie was never afraid of the ceremonial event and, as modest as he wanted to be, he was very willing to go along with the honor paid him "because it would help them raise more money." Dad brought home his plaques and diplomas and hung them all in a room in our basement, which I dubbed (with some malice) the "Ego Room." Dad, with some humor about himself, laughed and truly thought it was funny. A curious detail: in the "Ego Room" he also hung, mounted in picture frames, some hate letters he had received from some anti-Semites who also hated blacks. Hatred was also for him another form of personal recognition which encouraged him in his battle for justice.

This series of honors and dinners and awards continued to the end of his days, a worthy and important part of his life. It may have been the best way for people and organizations to show him their appreciation. But for the rest of the family, well. . . .

In a strange and beautiful way, these honors did not make him value his family less. On the contrary, his family remained for him the main source of satisfaction or sadness.

Seeking to integrate his public and private life, Dad always gave a life membership in the NAACP to new members of the family. He saved the glory of the fiftieth for my wife, Sandy, which he consecrated with a presentation picture with Mr. Roy Wilkins. When our son Jeremy Joshua was born, he became the youngest life member, at only ten hours old. When asked why he had waited so long, Kivie would reply that Jeremy was born right after midnight and he had to wait until the next day to register the baby.

When Kivie's children were becoming more independent, putting time into their own families and personal needs, Kivie became more and more open to young people (especially rabbis) and their wives and families and traveled more and more. His already voluminous correspondence increased, and he became a veritable computer system for bringing people with common interests together, writing letters and making calls to put people with problems in touch with people with possible solutions. He was always very generous with his advice. There was a whirlwind quality about his life which, despite more frequent bouts of sickness and exhaustion near the end, never showed signs of letting up. His tremendous need to help, to give, and to care carried him far beyond the immediate family, to the point that the world was his family, especially the liberal Jewish community and the black community.

But we were still part of that whirlpool. All anniversaries and birthdays were recognized with precision by a phone call and a check. Typical of Kivie: even our engagement anniversary (which we do not remember or celebrate) was an occasion for a card and a call, and, when we told him that it didn't mean anything for us, he told us we were "dead wrong" and gave us a little inspirational lecture for the same price. The greatest gift he could bestow upon us personally as children was to convince us of the truth of his formula for successful living.

In all this, a simple dimension is absent: what Martin Buber made famous as the "I-Thou" relationship. Pity was always strong in Kivie, a sense of empathy for the suffering and humiliation of others, prompting his generous assistance and sense of strength. But to recognize and understand a different approach to life was more difficult, and so we always remained children. It seems sometimes that he also sacrificed his inner life to the social task. He never enjoyed being alone, and he did not develop a sense of the inner life, of inner peace — a perfect example of Riesman's "outer-directed man." To forget the loneliness of the quiet moment, he buried the unspeakable in an endless stream of human contacts. Always thinking about what to do for so many people, he was often absent in the here and now. He was always excellent and responsive with little children, but, one day when we were watching my two-year-old son play in a yard, he suddenly took out his notepad and wrote a memo to himself: something to do tomorrow. Overwhelming himself and others with his ubiquity, he became like a prophet coming home to his family after a world tour.

Fortunately, Dad did not take himself as seriously as one might expect, and his drive was often tempered by detachment. A nonconformist in ethics according to the norm of middle-class America, he was also eccentric in other ways. Part of his identity was, of course, having money. Always reserving, as he said, thirty percent of his income for charity, he also used some of it for personal comfort. In his early days he would buy expensive suits, forty-dollar Sulka shirts, and special handmade shoes made of perforated calf suede; those shoes looked weird but were quite light and comfortable. He would also give his old clothes to Ralph Harlow to wear after he had outgrown them. In his later days, always subordinating style to comfort, he preferred cheaper clothing, which often looked baggy because of his fluctuations in weight. He did not mind looking sometimes like "a bum in the street," and he got a kick out of it, especially when mother criticized him for being shabby. He enjoyed the role of nonconformist; he applied this attitude to others and always stuck up for young men in beards and welcomed all forms of dissent — especially when it involved personal freedom.

He was a person who could produce shock for both moral and childish reasons, fleeing from neither. The child in him still did the trick of putting a mouthful of food on his tongue and sticking out said tongue at the dinner table, to tease mother and amuse me. He had an idiosyncratic system of word substitutions with which he delighted in teasing people: "rechetords" (records), "albumen" (album), "riser" (trip), "Good Shnubby-dubdubbess" (Good Shabbos), "choffy-toff" (coffee), "brechy-fast" (breakfast), and so on.

At social occasions, Kivie was always ready to sell life memberships in the NAACP, never embarrassed to trap people in their own contradictions. To black people he might say: "Look at my skin and look at yours. What have *you* done for the NAACP?" Every black should start to become a life member, fifty dollars a year for ten years, only fifteen cents a day, etc. To white people, to Jews especially, he would evoke the tragedy of the Jewish past and point out that if they have money they should share it. To some people, he would say directly: "You are a bigot." Sometimes the people would admit it. When approached by many white people who had problems with black housekeepers, he would answer, "You are confusing a domestic problem with social justice," and thus put them in their place. Kivie was never shy about being direct and challenging and preferred to have a few friends of high quality than a lot of friends, as he often said.

There was some ambiguity about Kivie. His almost uncanny instinct for spotting problems of social injustice and discrimination was coupled with a sometimes ruthless pragmatism, disregarding the inner conflicts of those he might confront. He was not exempt from a certain competitiveness, yet he obtained and gave relief with his humor and silly pranks. He always wanted to harmonize his family life with the numerous activities outside the home which preoccupied him; he did this mostly by bringing us into the world and by telling us about it. In that way his overweening dedication to social justice became an essential part of our relationship to him, and his vision of brotherhood became a part of our lives.

# 4

# Kivie as Businessman

## Saul Levine

*

M any successful businessmen present two faces to the world. One, the ruthless entrepreneur who probably has to force his way up in a highly competitive environment and who runs his business empire with an iron hand; the other, the devoted and loving family man known for his generosities and civic virtues in the bedroom suburb he calls home. Neither face is false, each is a true facet of a very real human being. Kivie Kaplan was cast in this mold.

Kivie was the youngest of the three Kaplan brothers who started the Colonial Tanning Company in 1924, specializing in the manufacture of patent leather, an item difficult to produce because it was prone to crack unless done with utmost care and yet more difficult to merchandise as its shiny look moved in and out of fashion's spotlight.

In the years of their greatest success the brothers loved to recount stories of their early trials and how Colonial was started, particularly the incident of "Papa's banker." In the beginning, Papa (B.J.) Kaplan had a small patent leather factory, of very limited success, and the boys worked for him. Papa was a proud and stubborn man and wasn't about to relinquish the reins to upstart sons whom he expected to obey him, not only because he was the boss, but also because he was Papa — and so the boys left to go it alone. Papa's banker, apparently a liberal and tolerant man for his day, gave the boys some vital bank credit so they could have their fling. Two years later, the story goes, the banker called in the boys, told them they had done very well, better than he had expected, but enough was enough; it was time to close up shop and return to help Papa. When they refused, he withdrew their bank credit to force the issue, but it was too late. Their brief but good beginning was enough to get them credit at another bank, and Colonial was firmly launched, the patriarchal umbilical cord permanently severed.

SAUL LEVINE *is president of General Split Corporation in Milwaukee.*

Colonial had reached the tender age of five years when the stock market crashed in 1929, and in the following years of the Great Depression many seasoned and substantial tanneries closed their doors. But to the surprise of many, and the consternation of the competition, Colonial under the guidance of Kivie and his brothers not only survived but grew and prospered. This would have been a rare feat for any company in those days, but in the patent leather business it was a near-miracle. The demand for patent leather had been shrinking year after year as it declined in popularity but, even as the industry's total volume shrank, Colonial's production and sales increased. By the mid-thirties it was producing more than fifty percent of all the patent leather made and sold in the United States, leaving in its wake many giants of the tanning industry.

How did these upstarts manage such a feat? In 1924 Kivie was twenty or twenty-one years old, the brothers just a few years older. They started with $12,000 capital, and ten years later were doing a multimillion-dollar business.

It is not possible to assess to what degree each brother was responsible for the overall success; but it is possible to ascribe to each the role he played. If brother Archie was the planner, Kivie was the doer; if brother Joe was the peripatetic ambassador of goodwill, Kivie stayed in the kitchen and took the heat. On a day-to-day basis, month in and month out, it was Kivie who ran the show. And the show was not run on sentiment. Kivie would win no popularity contests, neither from those who sold him hides nor from those who bought his leather. But he didn't try. He asked no quarter and gave none. Both hide suppliers and leather customers often complained at the ruthlessness of Colonial's methods, but none could question its honesty or integrity. Kivie's word was his bond, he spoke plainly without rhetoric or double-talk, and one always knew exactly where he stood. For these latter qualities he was appreciated by a few high-caliber customers and suppliers who held him in esteem and valued his friendship.

Only Colonial, of the patent leather tanners of the day, had the courage to stay in full production during good periods and bad. When patent was not in demand, Colonial sold at cost and below cost, driving prices down and competitors to despair. But employees of Colonial factories worked fifty-two weeks per year, their selling agents had fat commission checks twelve months per year, and customers with fortitude had cheap leather to make shoes with, without which they would have had to close their shoe factories. The whole world, literally, would be scoured by Colonial representatives to find customers who could be induced or seduced into placing orders to keep the tanning wheels turning. But when the fashion cycle would start to change, and patent came back into demand, Colonial would be the first to sense it, weeks ahead of the competition, and would have the momentum to anticipate and meet the demand. This is when the sparks would begin to fly. This is when Kivie would move to put some fat back into the corporate pocketbook grown a little lean. Like a general taking personal charge of a great battle, Kivie would watch the size, direction, and tempo of incoming orders. Increasing prices several times in a single day, testing the strength of demand by reaching for new highs, he never failed to know or sense when only Colonial could satisfy milady's new-found appetite for patent leather shoes and accessories. Ruthless is what customers called him, and ruthless he was. Woe betide the hapless buyer who hesitated or balked at a ten percent price increase; his hesitation might well cost him another fifteen percent!

Kivie enjoyed these periods, even though he took no little verbal abuse from irate customers. I am sure Kivie fancied himself at these times in a Robin Hood role — taking from the wealthy and returning (at least some) to charity.

Kivie and his brothers sat at desks in a single large, open office with stenographers, bookkeepers, clerks, and switchboard operators; a self-imposed austerity that did not permit a single private office in a firm doing $20 million plus in annual sales. Kivie spoke into an upright standing telephone with a Hush-a-Phone attachment for privacy that seemed to swallow half the face of the person speaking into it. For private conferences the brothers beckoned one another into an empty corner and spoke in whispers. If some of their privacy leaked out, they didn't miss much of what was going on around them either.

All the office employees were male — switchboard operator, secretaries, stenographers, bookkeepers, and clerks. It was part of their no-nonsense approach to business and continued until World War II forced a change. To many visitors it must have looked a little weird, but the all-male policy paid off handsomely as a means of training future executives. One vice-president of a major division got his start and early training as Kivie's secretary, and at least two more in similar menial jobs. It wasn't just the all-male policy; it was also the recruiting method. Each year the High School of Commerce (the Kaplans' alma mater) was invited to send up for employment interviews their top three or four graduates, and the most promising were given jobs. The result was that Colonial had the smartest young organization in the business, and it was known in the leather district that even those who failed to make the grade at Colonial usually did pretty well elsewhere.

One of the things that the Hush-a-Phone failed to keep from coming through was Kivie's fierce devotion to his wife and family. It was known, through people who knew him years earlier, that Kivie and Emily had been childhood sweethearts and presumably had married very young against parental opposition. It came through from this very reserved man that the love affair had never ended.

Another facet of Kivie's family relationships that intruded into his business life had to do with his father, B. J. Kaplan. It came about largely through B. J.'s matzah business, which he apparently started some time during his retirement and which he ran for a few weeks each year prior to the Passover holiday, using the Colonial headquarters as his own. His goateed visage, seen but infrequently the rest of the year, was a daily sight during the "season." He came through as a vain and stubborn man, alternately good-humored and irascible, whose attitude toward his sons seemed to vacillate between pride in their accomplishments and unforgiveness for their long-ago desertion. On their part, the sons' attitude toward their father seemed to contain a mixture of affection, tolerance, an outward attempt at filial respect, but also an ill-disguised measure of contempt. On the other hand, the rare visits of their mother revealed an uncomplicated love and devotion which continued during her considerable widowhood.

Kivie's concern for others was not without manifestations in his business life, but it largely involved what today would be called employer paternalism. Nevertheless, the annual employee outings to Canobie Lake Park in New Hampshire or the famous Toll House in Whitman, Massachusetts, were a wonderful relief from the drabness of those Depression times. And Kivie, the benefactor, a tremendous lover of food and of fun when he would permit himself, would probably admit to being the one who benefited most. At least, he certainly enjoyed himself as much as anyone there, playing the general camp leader, umpiring the games, eating more than most, and making sure a fair share of the goodies came home for the Kaplan tribe. And the bonuses, later called profit sharing, which could be as much as an extra week's pay each month for several months, or as little as nothing for an equal length of time, brought not only extra cash, but excitement, anticipation, joy, and disappointment, all in ample measure.

In the earlier years of the brothers' success, if they were called upon to use their considerable talents and energy in helping to raise funds for a worthy cause they espoused, Archie would say, "Let others work on the drives, we will concentrate on what we do best, making money and giving generously." In the early years Kivie went along with this philosophy. But it is perhaps a measure of the growth of this remarkable man that he moved from this position to one of greater and greater personal struggle and involvement in causes in which he believed, most especially that of the growing movement for equality of citizenship for black people. Eventually he changed direction completely, retiring from business and devoting his great ability and energy to what had to be, for a white man, a difficult and lonely cause.

The course of that long road, which took him to Selma and beyond, I know of only sketchily. He told me many times of the great influence on his thinking of Professor Ralph Harlow, who first interested him in the cause of black people and the NAACP; of how difficult and unrewarding it was in terms of the complete lack of understanding from his white friends; and of his determination because of and in spite of this to see it through if it took a lifetime.

At this time, carrying out his responsibilities as chairman of the NAACP's Life Membership Committee was paramount. Business associates were among his prime targets, and few escaped his bulldog tenacity. Many whom he signed up admittedly understood neither Kivie's motivation nor his cause. But to Kivie that was almost beside the point. He understood that his role was to provide the finances for others to use to further the organization's goals. If a few of his associates understood and appreciated his efforts, that was an extra bonus, welcome but not essential.

One of several such instances I was witness to stands out in my mind, perhaps because it was dissimilar to most, but also because it illustrates the catholicity of his approach to his task. It was the day of the big affair of the shoe and leather industry — the 210 Associates banquet at the Waldorf Astoria. The 210 Associates is the charitable organization whereby the industry takes care of its own, and the banquet is its main fundraising event. Kivie was involved in the arrangements, and that afternoon he asked me to accompany him to the ballroom on some last-minute details. After conferring a short while with the black headwaiter, Kivie asked if he were a life member of the NAACP. Upon learning he was not, Kivie, as usual, pulled out all stops. It was an odd confrontation, this rich white man lecturing a not-so-rich black man on his duty to his fellow black people. There were some protestations, but it was strictly no contest. The headwaiter at the Waldorf had joined the army of NAACP life members enrolled by Kivie Kaplan.

The events leading up to Kivie's retirement from business were not entirely of his own doing. Following one of the not infrequent quarrels among the three brothers, Archie was bought out by Kivie and Joe, ending in bitterness their association of over thirty years. Each brother had a strong will, and over the years disagreements were commonplace. However, majority rule could always break any impasse. When Archie left, there was no longer any tie breaker and the two remaining brothers quarreled more frequently and bitterly than ever. Outwardly healthy, the business suffered internally from low employee morale and a stalemate on all decision making.

The impasse was finally broken by Joe's death, and Kivie found himself sole owner and alone in command. For a while this new challenge stirred his old ardor for business, but it did not last. Increasingly he delegated key responsibilities to employees less able than himself. Perhaps the organization had suffered too much inner rot during the years of stalemate, and perhaps Kivie simply could not sustain his old interest. When a fire totally destroyed Colonial's major production unit, it was for Kivie not a disaster but a way out. He chose not to reinvest the insurance proceeds in a new plant and equipment, opting instead for liquidating and personal freedom of choice. In 1961 Colonial closed its doors, marking the end of a most remarkable business empire.

# 5

S. Ralph Harlow's Influence

*Rabbi and Mrs. Samuel Perlman*

\*

A LL over the world there are people who claim to have
been close friends of Kivie. When Ralph Harlow died
in 1972, it was noted that he too was a close friend of scores of
people, thousands of miles distant from one another. Empty
generalizations? Not at all, for both these men knew how to be
friends, as illustrated in depth in their own relationship. In
their association over a period of thirty-five years, they defined "friendship" as they worked, counseled, and relaxed together. The story about Kivie would be incomplete without a
description of how Ralph and he enriched one another's lives,
and in so doing extended the outreach of their work for justice
and peace. They did not have to work at friendship, for both
possessed the qualities that translate an acquaintanceship into
a bond that strengthens a person to grow in sensitivity and
effectiveness. Some of the highlights of that voluntary partnership are being shared here in the hope that the reader will be
enriched in contemplating how two remarkable spirits brought
joy and strength and fulfillment to each other. Those who
knew Kivie will recognize why they also can with honesty
say "my friend Kivie."

What would Ralph and Kivie have been without one another? When they met in Temple Emanuel in Boston, Kivie's
cousin was about to be married to Ralph's daughter. This
family tie, however, was only one of many shared interests
which inevitably would have drawn these men into the same
orbit. Ralph had been invited to Temple Emanuel to speak on
Palestine. Ralph, with his wife Marion, after several years in
educational work in Turkey, was deeply committed to work
on the problems of the Middle East. Their observation of oppressed minorities made them champion the struggle of the
oppressed of all creeds and colors.

Because of this, Ralph was an early supporter of the idea
of a Jewish homeland in what was then Palestine. He was one

RABBI SAMUEL PERLMAN *was director of the
B'nai B'rith Hillel Foundation at Boston University.*

of the founders of the Christian Pro-Palestine Committee. He was also on the Board of the NAACP. Kivie was not only an active Jew but also an outspoken champion of black people. Ten years earlier, when returning from a business trip to Central America, he and Emily saw a sign in Miami that read "No dogs or Jews allowed." The black taxi driver put his arm around Kivie's shoulder and said, "Don't feel bad, Mr. Kaplan, we Negroes can't go out after 8:30 P.M. or swim at these beaches." Kivie then began his historic association with the struggle for civil rights. Ralph later directed Kivie toward the NAACP, where he became a dynamic factor in that organization's numerical and financial growth. Thus when Ralph and Kivie met at Temple Emanuel they were each launched on a lifework of fighting for justice. They met as companions in commitment, not as teacher and pupil. Neither ever became the satellite of the other.

Both men also believed that the cause of justice is best served through reason, persuasion, and effective citizen participation in the government process. Prophetic in their individual and shared visions, they used the tools of peace to battle the forces of evil. They visited and wrote to congressmen and to the president, they approached strategic people who could influence lawmakers, they activated friends to join in letter writing or contacting congressional or community leaders. Each of them possessed "antennae" which sensed in what direction effort would be most effective. They helped one another by sharing their insights and quandaries and by joining forces for action. The action was not always to criticize or exhort; often it was to commend people who had taken risks for justice and to whom a word of recognition might keep alive the determination to continue the struggle. The volume of mail flowing from these men's desks was phenomenal. Kivie kept two full-time secretaries for his NAACP work alone and reserved a desk for Ralph in the Kaplan family business headquarters. How often we heard each of these men remark, "I have just written to Congressman ———, can you write also?"

Both men believed in approaching people directly. They were honest, courageous, and personally involved. They were not rabble-rousers, but activists who appealed to people's best emotions and thoughts.

A further quality of the Kivie-Ralph friendship was the deep, fundamental respect they had for one another which eliminated competitiveness. They could not harm one another. Even when priorities might differ, there was no antagonism but a desire to understand one another. Each man was curious about any new thought. For example, Ralph and Marion were interested in experiences they and others had which gave credence to the existence of extrasensory perception. They, therefore, attended seances and explored ways of making contact with people who had died. Although Kivie and Emily had not had this interest they wanted to know what their friends were discovering. It never became a "cause" for Kivie, but his respect for Ralph led him to distribute thousands of copies of Ralph's book, *Life after Death*. Their admiration was mutual. As one friend put it, "They each placed a halo on the other's head and it always remained shining." They could question and challenge but never belittle one another.

There was a wide divergence in the personal wealth of the two men, but they placed similar value on material possessions. Ralph was a college professor, Kivie a successful industrialist, but both regarded money as a trust, to be used to lighten the burdens of others. Ralph would sacrifice his own comfort to send a few dollars to some cause, and even when he was a guest at a restaurant he always found that the least expensive item on the menu was "just what I have been wanting." For Kivie, money was not to buy prestige but to help others find self-respect and self-support. How often we have heard him say, "Freedom isn't free," as he urged people to join in using their resources, large or small, to support the NAACP.

When Ralph wanted his students to be exposed to people holding differing viewpoints, Kivie established a fund upon which Ralph could draw to bring visiting lecturers to his classes in religion. Realizing that the influence of Ralph and Marion Harlow needed to be perpetuated at Smith College after Ralph's retirement, Kivie joined with former students and friends of the Harlows to establish a scholarship fund which would enable students who had an interest in the problems of minorities to attend Smith College. This living memorial was established while Marion and Ralph could have the satisfaction of knowing that their ideas and efforts were appreciated in a practical, enduring testimonial. Because money was regarded as a trust, and not a private privilege to be squandered, the vast difference in economic status never ruffled the friendship. It was simply another resource to be used to promote their mutual concerns.

The distribution of books became a major expenditure for Kivie. When a new book on Israel or civil rights or a biography of a person such as Medgar Evers, Martin Luther King, Jr., or Abba Eban appeared, if Ralph felt it was worthwhile, Kivie could buy several hundred, sending them to people who could read them and promote the ideas still further. Money was used to combat ignorance and prejudice and at the same time to increase the royalties of the authors, helping them to continue their work. Ralph had the time and the background to assess the contents of the book, and Kivie provided the promotion. Ralph's philosophy has been helpful to hundreds of people through Kivie's distribution of Ralph's little volume, *Thoughts for Times like These*. Words of inspiration and challenge suggested by Ralph were printed on the back of Kivie's famous "Keep Smiling" and "Peace" cards and read appreciatively by thousands of people. It was a partnership of talents which spread knowledge and interest in immeasurable quantities, at the same time that the partnership provided encouragement to writers for social justice.

There was a trusting relationship between Kivie and Ralph, a twist of emotional as well as rational responses. For example, Marion and Ralph discovered a young lady in Greece who, having fled the Nazis, was once more in danger of being engulfed by the holocaust as it spread to the Near East. A brief cable to Kivie stating the need for $300 brought an instant response. How fortuitous that action was! Decades later, some years after Ralph lost his beloved Marion, he married Elizabeth, that very refugee whom Kivie and the Harlows had helped rescue from nazism. She brought Ralph renewed vigor and associations which enriched and prolonged his last years.

Ralph and Kivie did not need to approach one another gingerly with fear of being misunderstood, for their gut emotional responses were similar. They were incensed and inspired by the same events. We remember how they supported one another's pleas for social action, and we also remember their sonorous, jolly renditions of folk songs at the traditional Sunday night sings at the Harlows' home on Martha's Vineyard. We remember the Fourth of July community picnics by the Vineyard lagoon where the festive occasion became a rededication to the "self-evident truths that all men are created equal, that they are endowed by their Creator with certain inalienable rights, that among these are life, liberty, and the pursuit of happiness." They went together to the famous bridge at Concord, Massachusetts, where Ralph and Marion had become engaged. Once again Ralph recited Longfellow's memorial to those early brave revolutionaries. No wonder these men trusted one another! Whether picnicking with friends, or dining at a country club, or singing folk songs, or sharing a platform, or traveling alone or together, they delighted in the same human achievements, suffered over the same human indignities, and reacted in the same manner.

In addition to trusting one another's emotional responses, Kivie and Ralph also expected much of each other. No friendship can survive without mutual input of effort and cultivation. Ralph brought to Kivie his contacts and experiences with the academic and Christian community, while Kivie brought to Ralph his business acumen and the fruit of his lifelong involvement with Jewish religious and communal organizations. Kivie gave his friend entree to Jewish groups which enlarged his understanding of the Palestinian and later the Israeli situation. Beyond that, these two men (and their wives) kept in touch with one another not only to make requests or discuss problems but even just to say "Hello." When Kivie had difficult family problems, Ralph voluntarily undertook to assuage the hurts, and, when illness brought years of anxiety to the Harlows, Kivie and Emily were there in person or by telephone day after day. The travels of each were enriched by the contacts supplied by the other.

Many of us came to know Kivie through Ralph, and Kivie in turn delighted in bringing his friends to Ralph. Ralph introduced Kivie to Roger Baldwin, the president of the American Civil Liberties Union, and it was at the Harlow home that Kivie met Abba Eban, then Israeli representative to the United Nations and ambassador to the United States. Kivie knew scores of rabbis and brought them to Ralph's home where they enjoyed vigorous discussions of religious and current events. How real friendship creates responsibilities and mutual expectations was demonstrated to perfection by Kivie and Ralph.

Finally, the quality of the relationship between Ralph and Kivie was nurtured in the lifelong religious dedication of these two men. Ralph, the devout Christian, and Kivie, the devout Jew, found their inspiration and ethical guidelines in their respective faiths. "What doth the Lord require of thee but to do justly, to love mercy, and to walk humbly with thy God?" "Blessed are the meek — Blessed are the merciful — Blessed are they who hunger and thirst after righteousness — Blessed are the peacemakers." These were the precepts instilled in the young minds and spirits which later blossomed into great dedication to social reform. The source of each man's inspiration was religious and not political, and from childhood actions were measured by ethical principles, not individual gain.

Both Kivie and Ralph respected one another's religious

affiliations and were so ecumenical in their interpretation of their faiths that they sought membership in one another's religious institutions. It was not an empty gesture on Ralph's part when he asked to join a temple — not to become a Jew but to join the congregation in its struggle to understand and promote the prophetic teachings of Judaism. His respect for the "Judeo" part of his Judeo-Christian heritage was so great that he and Marion conducted Passover seders in their own home for Jewish students at Smith College and initiated the request for a Hillel counselor at the school. Ralph felt that two of the greatest honors of his lifetime were the honorary doctorates bestowed upon him by the Jewish Theological Seminary and the Hebrew Union College — Jewish Institute of Religion. It was Kivie who urged these institutions to honor his friend's fruitful dedication to the principles and practice of Judaism. Similarly, Kivie found no conflict with his own faith when as a member of a Congregational church he helped the congregation demonstrate how a black pastor could minister to the needs of a white community.

The prophetic tradition, with its emphasis on the promotion of social justice, was a mutual bond between this Jew and this Christian. The quality of their characters and judgment was rooted in their respective religious heritages. Small wonder it endured and was intensified by the onslaughts of personal and world tragedies! Together they mourned man's inhumanity to man, and together they resolved not to cease or desist from the struggle. To Kivie and to Ralph religion provided faith that a better world could and must be achieved, and it was also the source of the principles by which man would bring about such a better world. With such faith there was no room for cynicism or self-seeking, only for optimistic and optimum performance.

In paying tribute to the friendship of Kivie and Ralph, we affirm our own belief in the inevitability of a better world if friends demonstrate the same quality of relationship and motivation which these men exemplified. Between true friends there is a cooperative spirit in which each individual is free to be his finest self, not a merging or engulfing of one by the other, but a mutual supporting of constructive emotions and goals.

# 6

# Kivie the Jew

## *Roland B. Gittelsohn*

*

For crying out loud, it's about time you awakened to the fact that you are a Jew first and that Jewish rights and needs must be foremost and utmost.

Kivie Kaplan, the rich Jew . . . is now president of the National Association for the Advancement of Colored People. . . . Yearly the NAACP awards the Jewish Spingarn medal to Negroes and Jews for Race-Mixing and other Communist activities.

Get off your backside and fight for Jewish rights, or are you too ashamed to fight for your own people?

Big-mouth Kivie the Jew! Spending the winter in Florida with the money he makes on us dumb Negroes. We are happy here. If you don't keep your big mouth shut, we will do it for you.

THESE quotations, typical of many others written to or about Kivie Kaplan, effectively frame the dilemma as to his Jewishness. Anti-Semites harbored no doubts on the matter; they never referred to his civil rights activities without abusing him as a Jew. Some of his coreligionists were equally sure that in his devotion to the cause of blacks he all but obliterated his Jewish identity.

Kivie himself would have been the first to agree that any attempt to answer the bigots would be an exercise in futility. He would, moreover, be dismayed had he never been branded a Communist. That would signal that he had done nothing of any social consequence in his lifetime.

---

ROLAND GITTELSOHN *is rabbi of Temple Israel, Boston, and a past president of the Central Conference of American Rabbis.*

The quickest and easiest answer to his Jewish detractors — though it wasn't likely to dissuade them much more than a recital of facts will impress the others — was to list his very extensive Jewish affiliations and involvements. He was a founder of two congregations — one Orthodox, the other Conservative — remained a member of both and served as a life trustee of the latter. For thirty years he was a member of our Reform congregation, Temple Israel of Boston, where shortly before his death he was elected an honorary trustee for life. Kivie's congregational loyalties persisted even when he was technically on vacation. Over the course of thirty-three summers he became a bulwark of the Martha's Vineyard Hebrew Center, encouraging its members to pay off their mortgage, to purchase a permanent reservoir of prayer books, to join the Union of American Hebrew Congregations. The following comments by two charter members of the center attest to Kivie's Jewish activity at a time when he might reasonably have been expected to relax:

Kivie Kaplan is a giant in his concern for humanity and for exemplifying the tenets of his Judaism. . . .

He and his wife, Emily, take pride that during the thirty-three summers they have visited Martha's Vineyard they have not missed a single Friday evening service and other center activities.

Kivie personifies my concept of the total Jew. . . . He is not just a nominal Jew, giving lip service. To me, he is a Jew in that tradition of our prophets.

No major personal event in the life of my family ever occurred without notification that in honor of the occasion Emily and Kivie had made a contribution to one of their favorite philanthropies, more often than not the Jewish Memorial Hospital. Other close friends regularly enjoyed the same experience. In our own congregation the Kaplans created a Social Action Fund so that our work in this important area need not be always restricted to monies available through the temple budget.

The quality of Kivie's giving was further attested by his

response when the president of our congregation and I called on him and Emily at the outset of our building fund drive in 1971. His customary cordiality did not surprise us. We were amazed and delighted, however, when he cut us short almost at the beginning of our presentation to assure us that he was well aware of the need and it was not necessary to waste on him time which might better be directed to others. He proceeded to tell us that he wanted very much to pledge more than his charitable budget would allow for the announced period of our campaign and proposed to double that amount if we could arrange for a longer span for payment. Then, in a parting gesture which neither the president nor I will ever forget, he said: "I know from experience that you fellows are going to meet up with many heartaches and discouragements as you proceed with this drive. Don't let the stinkers discourage you. There will be many pleasant surprises, too, and I have no doubt that in the end you will succeed."

I trust that I would not be betraying Kivie's confidence in disclosing the fact that upon his retirement from active business he annually donated to philanthropies sixty percent of his income plus a portion of capital. Of these contributions, approximately three-fourths went to Jewish causes.

All this, while impressive, is far from a complete catalog of Kivie's Jewishness. In the history of the civil rights movement in the United States, there have been many descendants of Jews who have been motivated, if at all, only peripherally and unconsciously by Judaism. Their Jewish affiliations, moreover, are for all practical purposes nonexistent. Probably their children, certainly their grandchildren, will not even be aware of any Jewish origins.

Not so with Kivie. The original impetus for his interest in the NAACP came consciously and directly from his Jewish awareness. That hotel sign in Miami Beach reading "No dogs or Jews allowed" was the inception of Kivie's passion for the underdog. By touching the sensitive nerve of his own Jewishness, it awakened him to concern for all who are underprivileged or oppressed. From the outset, and at a time when such behavior was almost scandalous, the workers in the plant operated by him and his brothers were integrated. They also benefited from one of the first genuine profit-sharing plans in American industry. Even if others of limited vision have sometimes doubted, Kivie was always aware of the Jewish component in all this. He has said and repeated many times: "I feel I'm practicing my Judaism in my everyday life."

The last person in the world to allow the record to be contaminated with exaggeration would have been Kivie Kaplan himself. Painting him as a devoutly pious Jew from childhood on would have insulted his integrity. Though he grew up in a practicing Orthodox home, his Jewish education was minimal. He recalled studying just about enough Hebrew to celebrate his bar mitzvah. As an adult he followed the Hebrew in his prayer book, without pretending that he really understood all of it. Some years back, he spurned nomination as president of a Conservative congregation, saying that he would deem it a "fraud" for one of such limited Hebrew knowledge to assume such high congregational office. Among his memories of childhood was being "turned off" by a fervent "*davener*" who participated in daily synagogue services with exaggerated fervor but was known throughout the community as an unethical scoundrel. Like so many others, Kivie made the mistake of supposing that the alternatives he faced were of an either/or nature. He long ago matured to the point of understanding intellectually and demonstrating by his conduct that it is not a case of synagogue worship *or* ethical behavior; the ideal is to combine both. This combination he achieved with extraordinary skill.

What better way to judge the depth of Judaism in any person's life than by its functional meaning to his children? Perhaps without even articulating his hopes verbally, Kivie seemed determined to correct the deficiencies in his own Jewish education by doing better with his two daughters and his son. The girls attended a Conservative religious and Hebrew

school. Their brother observed his bar mitzvah in our Reform
congregation. Because almost immediately thereafter he left
Boston to study at a boarding school in western Massachusetts,
it was impossible for him to attend the regular sessions of his
confirmation class; I was thereby deprived of the privilege of
instructing him personally. I did confirm him, however; he
is one of the very few students over the course of more than
twenty years who actually completed his confirmation studies
in absentia. Without being unduly dictatorial or aggressive,
his parents made it clear that this was an obligation they expected him to fulfill. He did.

What do Sylvia, Jean, and Edward remember of their
childhood Jewish experiences? I asked them; their answers
are revealing. Aside from memories revolving around their
Jewish schooling, they recall annual expeditions to collect
funds for the Jewish National Fund. Kivie always supple-
mented their totals generously before they were turned in.
Chanukah was celebrated at Grandma Kaplan's. Kivie was
always involved in campaigns for both the Combined Jewish
Appeal and the United Fund. At times the kids were disturbed
by what appeared to them to be the heavyhanded methods
used to encourage more generous contributions to these causes.
The passage of time and their own active participation in
similar work have mitigated the harshness of their earlier
criticisms. They now understand what had bothered them.

Sylvia and Morton were married by an Orthodox rabbi,
a Conservative rabbi, and a cantor. Only the death of Joshua
Loth Liebman two weeks earlier excluded a Reform rabbi
from participation also. The nature of the officiants reflected
the respect for tradition as well as the Jewish eclecticism of
both groom and Kivie who maintained memberships in congregations representing all three major religious branches of
American Judaism.

All of Kivie's children — now adults with children of
their own — are closely and actively identified with the Jewish
community. One daughter and her husband are affiliated with

a Conservative congregation; the other couple belong to both Conservative and Reform synagogues; both practice the home rituals of Judaism with exceptional beauty. It was a rare delight to share Shabbat dinner with Emily and Kivie, surrounded by an assortment of children and grandchildren. Edward — my in absentia confirmand and now a professor of Romance languages at Amherst College — developed a close personal friendship during his student years with the late Abraham Joshua Heschel. He has written of Heschel with poetic sensitivity and has published profound articles on Jewish religious experience.

One of the most beautiful wedding ceremonies at which I have officiated in my thirty-seven years as a rabbi was that which united the lives of Kivie's eldest granddaughter Amy and the son of my congregation's president. In his own right, Richard Narva — a founder of *Response* magazine — has become an extremely thoughtful critic and supporter of the Jewish community. The *chupah* at their ceremony, embroidered by Emily, symbolized Shabbat and all other festive occasions of the Jewish year. Without detracting an iota from the credit due Amy's parents — Sylvia and Morton Grossman — it is obvious that the deep Jewish religious loyalties of Amy's grandparents had more than a little to do with the positive Jewish posture she and Richard have assumed. Equally pervasive was the influence of the senior Kaplans on Amy's twin, Louis. More recently married to another of my confirmands, in his own way he promises no less as a practicing, participating Jew.

In a lifetime replete with well-earned gratifications, few experiences brought greater joy to Emily and Kivie than the Eisendrath-International-Exchange Scholarship our congregation awarded several years ago to their granddaughter Linda. Her sister Rachel, one of my prize confirmands of 1973, is now enrolled in our postconfirmation department. "And see thou the good of Jerusalem all the days of thy life; and see thy children's children."

The least publicized but perhaps most significant phase of Kivie Kaplan's Jewishness was his relationship to rabbis. There may well have been no other layman in the country with so many rabbinical friends or so much deep concern for their welfare. On his very extensive travels, this man, whose Judaism was so often maligned, carried with him a copy of the *Alumni Directory* of the Hebrew Union College–Jewish Institute of Religion, so that in every community he visited he might telephone the incumbent Reform rabbi and, if possible, host him and his wife for dinner. Again, the roots of childhood flowered as Kivie in turn extended his parents' hospitality to "an endless stream" of rabbis who visited their home.

Even with rabbis who were strangers to him, even with those who were not notably active on the civil rights front, Kivie took the heartache of each unto himself. Rare indeed was the layperson — leader of a congregation or of our union of congregations — who empathized so fully with rabbis. I know the details of one incident in which a colleague's troubles were attributable at least as much to his own inadequacies as to those of the congregation. Kivie saw the situation not as one calling for assignment of blame but as the intense suffering of a man and his family. That suffering had to be alleviated. No one will ever know the number of long-distance telephone calls, the miles traveled, the individuals contacted at length, the time and concern expended by Kivie, until finally a substantial measure of justice and rehabilitation was achieved both for the man and the congregation. All this, without any publicity — indeed, under the shield of confidentiality.

Each of the many young rabbis who came in succession through the years to assist me was immediately befriended by Emily and Kivie, often even before his arrival in Boston. The usual routine included packages of "goodies," bundles of books, generous dinner invitations, and ears always attuned to the worries of a young rabbi or his wife.

Kivie probably involved himself in counseling as many persons contemplating intermarriage as has the average rabbi.

More than a few individuals of both sexes have been persuaded to become Jews before marrying, persuaded both by
Kivie's words and by the vivid example he provided of how
a modern Jew can live his or her Judaism. And where parents
were reluctant to accept a prospective son or daughter-in-law,
with or without conversion, Kivie did not hesitate to intervene,
to impress upon such a person the obligations imposed upon
him by both Jewish tradition and human compassion.

Kivie's frequent addresses to widely scattered chapters
of the NAACP were always matters of public notice. What
remained largely unknown was that in nearly every instance he
tried to arrange in advance to meet with a Jewish group in
the same community, to impress upon them that part of their
Jewish heritage which should impel them to seek justice for
the "stranger," for they should know from their own psychic
trauma what a "stranger" must endure. His constant message
to the timorous and insecure among his fellow Jews was that
they cannot be free until all men and women are free. It
pleased him immensely that invitations to speak before Jewish
audiences came much more frequently in later years. The hate
mail continued. Epithets were hurled in his direction. But
there was a slowly growing acceptance and respect, too, even
in parts of the country where the name of Kivie Kaplan
was anathema among Jews of little knowledge or faith.

From time to time in this account — though my assignment was to write only about Kivie — it has been impossible not
to couple Emily's name with his. None of Kivie's accomplishments through the years — Jewish or otherwise — could have
been attained without his beloved Emily. Other wives have
objected strenuously when their husbands traveled only a
fraction of Kivie's time away from home, and when no
jeopardy to their personal safety was involved. It would be
inhuman to assume that Emily has not had her moments of
loneliness, of doubt, of fear. But she never permitted them to
interfere with what her husband interpreted to be the divine
imperative of his life. No man could follow a career so prophetic

and productive as this without imposing a price on his family. In willingly paying that price, Emily and their children became partners to the vast good that was accomplished.

But her share was much more than merely passive endurance. Though she is essentially a shy and retiring person, though she encouraged her husband to be the spokesman for both family and causes, Emily in her steadfast, quiet way shared all of Kivie's concerns fully. To know this, one had but to watch her face, peer into her eyes, when Kivie was the recipient of public honor or praise. She has been indeed an *"eshet chayil."*

Near the close of 1972, at the request of Maurice Eisendrath and Alexander Schindler, Kivie Kaplan represented the Union of American Hebrew Congregations when the Conference of Presidents of Major American Jewish Organizations met with high government officials in Israel. There Kivie served a purpose which no one in the world was as qualified as he to perform. He tried to help Israelis understand how extravagantly exaggerated their impression is of black anti-Semitism in the United States. He said: "The time has come to place this in proper context. Only a tiny minority of blacks are bearers of the cancer of anti-Semitism. The major reservoirs of anti-Semitism in this country are still white Christian." This is a matter both of morality and of potential practical benefit to Israel, he insisted, "since most blacks are favorable to Jews and Israel, and blacks represent a major public opinion resource for Israel."

Here at home Kivie consistently served the reverse function of interpreting the Jewish community to blacks — and of warning his fellow Jews not to indulge in the unjustified luxury of self-righteousness. True, he admitted there had been some increase of anti-Semitism among blacks. But there had been no less a trend toward antiblack sentiment among Jews. Neither was excusable. Neither escaped scathing indictment by this most extraordinary man.

Kivie the Jew. Kivie the advocate of social action. Kivie

the prophet who lived to see his noblest aspirations and dreams — though still threatened and in peril — at least partially realized. Can these variant aspects of one human being be neatly compartmentalized? As chapters in a book, yes. In life itself, no. Neither Kivie nor any of us who admired and loved him could really tell where his Judaism began or ended. Yet we know that it existed as one of the most compelling and pervasive forces in his career.

# 7

# The Man with a Heart

## *Herman Pollack*

*

In the messianic age the Holy One, blessed be He, will bring the "evil inclination" [the forces of evil] and slay [destroy] it in the presence of the righteous and the wicked. To the righteous it will have the appearance of a towering hill, and to the wicked it will have the appearance of a hair thread. Both the former and the latter will weep. The righteous will weep, saying [questioning]: "How were we able to surmount such a high hill?" The evil will weep, saying [questioning]: "How is it that we were unable to conquer this hair thread?"

(Talmud, Sukah 52a)

If there is need for both a synagogue and a lodging-place for the poor, let the community build the lodging-place first.

(Yehudah he-Chasid, *Sefer Chasidim*, Berlin, 1891, sec. 1529, pp. 374–75)

KIVIE Kaplan must not be described by the conventional term philanthropist. True, he was interested in and supported various religious and educational organizations, Jewish and non-Jewish humanitarian causes. But foremost in his mind was the furtherance of justice, even if it required challenging the established order, or "the power structure," as Kivie was apt to put it. More appropriately, Kivie was the philanthropist with the spirit of a rebel who wished to transform society as it exists. His concern that human misery be brought to an end stemmed from a heart that had no rest so long as even one person suffered.

In the summer of 1951 I heard about Kivie for the first time from Rabbi Benjamin Lowell who was then serving as rabbi of the congregation in Havana, Cuba. During the hysteria in the era of Senator Joseph McCarthy of Wisconsin, after Ben lost his rabbinical posts, he became rabbi of the Havana congregation. Often there were visitors at the Shabbat services and he had the opportunity to greet many guests from the United States. One Friday evening Emily and Kivie Kaplan introduced themselves. From the outset Kivie asked,

HERMAN POLLACK *is emeritus rabbi and director of B'nai B'rith Hillel Foundation at MIT. He teaches at Boston University.*

"Why are you here?" And Kivie continued, with a twinkle of the eye, "You must have been a bad boy!" As Ben related it:

I told him the whole story: first, how I lost my pulpit in Montgomery, Alabama, for defending the young men in the Scottsboro case; how I then worked in California as a laborer and as a technician in the movie industry; how I was placed in the National Hillel office as the assistant to the director; and then how I lost my position with Hillel and my weekend congregation in Jackson, Queens, New York, because I supported the Hollywood Ten. But Kivie was not impatient with me. He was in no hurry. What apparently aroused him was when I told that a Reform Jewish leader said that I was too controversial and nothing more could be done for me. Kivie answered, "I shall pursue the matter and learn why you were thrown on the scrapheap."

Ben told how his spirits were uplifted by his visit with this layman of such unusual social sensitivity and concern for the welfare of others. Shortly after Ben met Kivie, he passed away.

About two years later, after we moved to Boston, I met Kivie at a gathering in the home of a colleague. I told Kivie that we already knew him through Ben Lowell. Kivie said, "It is too bad Ben died so young. I recognized that he was no ordinary person. He had my respect for having the courage of his convictions."

A few days after, Kivie called and invited me to his business, the Colonial Tanning Company, to join him for lunch. I expected a private office bearing Kivie's name on the door, but to my surprise I found him in a large room with perhaps thirty or forty other persons. I was reminded of the newspaper room where city editors, rewrite staff, reporters, and copy carriers are jostled together working in the same area. This business executive was no bureaucrat hidden inside an office while guarded on the outside by a staff of secretaries.

For lunch we went a short distance to a cafeteria that was part of the company. Employers and employees were eating in the same room. I was skeptical: Could this be a device whereby workers forget the class differences between themselves and their employer? I tried to probe and asked Kivie: "Where do you eat lunch when you have a business engagement?" He answered, "Here! Let them learn a lesson of democracy at work. We have an open policy on employment; there is no discrimination of any kind. We have workers who are black and Orientals. For a short time," Kivie added, "and only for a short time, we did not employ women, but we reversed this policy." Kivie, continuing his remarks, said, "The meals are free to the employees." Then he explained that each worker was part of a profit-sharing program that was introduced after the business was started in 1924. Obviously, Kivie was not the usual industrialist for whom financial gain was the primary concern.

Since that day I sought to learn more about Kivie, about the influences in his own life that made him so deeply concerned with regard to social issues and so passionately involved in eliminating human oppression and misery.

One day I asked Kivie the origin of his name. He said, "I was named for an ancestor in my family, Rabbi Akiva." I was curious to know if bearing the name of Akiva — the famous talmudic teacher who challenged the oppressive policies of the Roman government — could have had an influence on him. Kivie did not wish to speculate, but instead he singled out specific instances in his boyhood and youth, as if saying: Here are the roots of my values.

In his early years, Kivie told me, he learned about the realities of human existence — about the hardships and insecurities people face and about their daily struggles for survival. He observed how his mother, Celia (née Solomont),* befriended and helped those in need, regardless of race, color, or creed. For thirty-seven years she was president and treasurer of the Jewish Women's Convalescent Home. The institution, Kivie explained, served poor people who were discharged from hospitals but not yet well enough to go home.

Once, when his mother was walking with him on the

* The Talmud Torah in Malden, Massachusetts, Bet Solomon, was named for Kivie's grandfather Solomon Solomont.

street, they met a homeless man. Kivie said that he shuddered and wanted to pass him, but his mother, insisting that this destitute person should not be rejected, stated emphatically: "Were you to give to twenty-five such persons, and only one was worthy, you are still ahead." Kivie also recalled the incident of money having been set aside to buy new clothes for Rosh Hashanah and Pesach, but his mother, instead, used the money to assist those in dire straits in his neighborhood. Such acts of human kindness no doubt served as a model for his conduct.

Kivie reminisced further how his boyhood environment — living among people who cared for one another and were sensitive to one another's problems — shaped his outlook. From the very beginning, his life was connected with communal service. At the time of his *bris*, his father, Benjamin Julius, was one of the founders of the Adas Yeshurun Shul on Blue Hill Avenue in Boston.* This event, which Kivie learned about from his father, also had an effect in singling out the goals that would have his allegiance.

Furthermore, Kivie recounted, his father had one of the longest lists of *meshulochim* who collected funds for Jewish institutions and causes. They came from Palestine, Europe, and the United States, and from them Kivie — then between the age of eight to ten — was made aware of Jewish needs. As a result of such exposure, Kivie, at the age of twenty, became interested in Jewish philanthropies and causes.

Through the influence of his grandfather, Rabbi Kaplan, he derived a flexible, liberal orientation to Judaism. When Kivie said to his grandfather, "I wish to understand the meaning of the Hebrew prayers," his grandfather immediately provided him with a Hebrew and English edition of the prayer book. Kivie acknowledged that his grandfather's conduct — in not dismissing him when he expressed this concern — served as an effective object lesson not to disregard the needs of others.

---

* Kivie tells that his grandfather Rabbi Chomelyah Kaplan often took him to attend services in the Blue Hill Avenue Shul.

These values which were part of his childhood were later given expression by him in a variety of ways: in his devoted concern to further the development and well-being of Jewish life; in his passionate espousal of justice for all blacks and all oppressed minority groups; in his concern for and defense of "the little people" who became crushed by the wheels of our economic system; in his interest in social action and social change; in his warmhearted friendship shown rabbis, especially when they were threatened for expressing their social concerns and for taking controversial stands; and in his support of unpopular causes. Kivie devoted the fullest measure of his own strength and idealism to each of these areas.

In 1962, at the age of fifty-eight, he retired from business to give all of his time to the crucial causes that were more and more enveloping his life. At the age of seventy-one he continued to make great demands on himself by carrying a heavy schedule.

Again, I emphasize that this account is not about a philanthropist who was motivated by the desire to plug the holes in our leaking social structure or to cover up with Band-Aids the wounds caused by the ravages of our economic system. In no way would we find Kivie, the retired industrialist, an apologist for any of the injustices or inequities that result from predatory, greedy practices on our society.

If one asked Kivie what he had done in the Boston Jewish community that he considered to be among his important accomplishments, he would refer to the twenty-seven years that he served the Jewish Memorial Hospital in various capacities, including that of treasurer and chairman of the endowment fund. If one asked what had attracted him to this institution for the chronically ill, he said with no hesitation: "It was a poor people's hospital. . . . I support the underdog. . . . Even in philanthropy the influences of the upper and lower classes can be noticed. I am on the side of the lower classes every time." He had been made honorary treasurer of the hospital, no doubt in recognition of all that he did, especially in establishing buildings and a substantial endowment fund.

A written report of an officer of the hospital described the arduous labor in which Kivie engaged so as to obtain support for their cause:

He [Kivie] had a motion picture made of the general work that the hospital did. . . . Kivie Kaplan and I used to go from house to house to some of our so-called prominent citizens. One of us would lug the projector in and the other would carry the screen [and films], and we would show the picture to the prospect. In most cases, we got results, not as much as we thought we should get.

Apparently, they never despaired but "kept smiling," and over the years personal contact and face-to-face discussion had a cumulative effect. Kivie always used the same approach: He first acquainted an individual with a problem of immediate concern and then elicited his or her support in behalf of a project to solve it.

On the occasion of his fiftieth birthday, Kivie Kaplan was honored by the Jewish Memorial Hospital. The citation reads: "A merchant prince of outstanding talent and integrity; his great heart has made mercy, kindness, and love of humanity the guiding motivation of his life. He has been a shining light of modesty and of never ceasing concern for the sick, the poor, the unfortunate."

Kivie's philanthropic interests and human concerns cannot be separated, for both merged and became a unity as he struggled for social betterment. His deep interest in social action was for the purpose of affecting needed changes. Abuses in our society, he stated, will not disappear by the wave of a magic wand of good will. The conscience of the people will have to be aroused so that they will call for change.

As a member of the Social Action Commission of the Union of American Hebrew Congregations, Kivie fostered the development of social action committees in local congregations. On his trips he spoke to congregations and met with rabbis to encourage them to speak out on the social problems of the day, and where they found themselves in the lonely minority he suggested how they might gain more allies and support. But, in his awareness of the forces congregations and rabbis must contend with in their communities, he called upon them not to be frightened and not to make compromises.

"Compromising long enough," so Kivie contended, "will result in betrayal — our betraying what Judaism stands for."

When Kivie was criticized for being too involved in non-Jewish issues and for urging rabbis and congregations to be interested in general social, political, and economic affairs, he replied that, the more individuals take their Judaism seriously, the more must they concern themselves with human problems. In this regard he related that when he took part in a picket line sponsored by the NAACP in front of the Woolworth store in St. Paul, Minnesota, protesting discrimination in hiring blacks, he was told: "As a big business man, your conduct was beneath your dignity." Unruffled and unperturbed, his answer was: "If you believe, you believe."

Kivie's leadership in the Reform Jewish movement, both in and outside America, was reflected in the positions he occupied. They were not mere positions of honor, as they involved considerable effort and time because of the correspondence and travel involved. He was vice-chairman of the UAHC and had been elected its honorary life chairman, only the second time such an honor had been accorded in a hundred years. As a member of the North American Board of the World Union for Progressive Judaism, he maintained contact with Jewish leaders on several continents. He continued to be the gadfly with probing questions and challenging statements for Kivie did not cater to or curry the favor of those in high places. He did not hesitate to needle, challenge, and annoy those in leadership with the question: Why do Jews in South Africa capitulate to apartheid? For Kivie there was no evil as horrendous as racism.

Kivie's identity with Jewish religious life was as all-embracing and as total as was his view of justice. Orthodox and Conservative congregations were not considered by him to be secondary because of his involvements in the Reform movement. He adhered to the principle that the Jewish com-

munity transcends parochialism and single-minded denomina-
tionalism. Yet it was his concern that no religious group,
Orthodox, Conservative, or Reform, should become self-
righteous and bigoted and out of an exaggerated sense of
importance assert that it — and it alone — represents "true
Judaism." As one would anticipate, his circle of Jewish life
was all-inclusive, within which there was the secularist, the
nonreligious person who incorporated into his or her own life
the history, teachings, and observances of Judaism. The
secularist must be part of the Jewish community; otherwise,
Kivie maintained, we do not uphold freedom of conscience for
the individual.

A review of some of Kivie's activities will show how he
put into practice an all-inclusiveness of approach which was
concerned with encouraging and aiding each group to fulfill
itself in accordance with its beliefs and convictions. It was
through his initiative that the Orthodox *shul*, Anshe Shalom,
was established in Ayer, Massachusetts, some twenty-five
years ago. The synagogue was dedicated in honor of Emily and
Kivie Kaplan, and Kivie remained a member of the congregation. He served on the Traditional Institutions Committee of
the Combined Jewish Philanthropies of Boston. The committee included Orthodox and Conservative rabbis and laypersons.
Furthermore, he was an honorary life trustee of the Reform
congregation of Temple Israel of Boston and was co-founder
and life trustee of the Conservative congregation of Temple
Emanuel of Newton, Massachusetts.

On his travels Kivie constantly spoke to congregations at
their Sabbath services on the theme of applying the ethics of
Judaism. Hence when he became president of the NAACP,
Rabbi Joseph Kamenetsky, national director, *Torah Umeso-
rah*, the central body for Orthodox day schools, sent Kivie a
congratulatory message for practicing Judaism.

Two awards were among his collection of honors showing the personal ties he had with synagogues. One was
the 1969 Human Rights Award during Chanukah 5730, from
Temple Sharey Shalom, Springfield, New Jersey, on which is

mounted the "Dove of Peace." The other was a Bible printed in Tel Aviv, which was presented on Kislev 5728 (December 8, 1967) by the Brotherhood Synagogue in New York City; the inscription refers to the "inspiring leadership in the struggle for human dignity" rendered by "Kivie Kaplan, National President, NAACP." To Kivie, the importance of these awards was the recognition that the Jewish heritage is deeply concerned about the problems of daily life.

When he was told that a congregation refused to enroll children in its Hebrew school because the family could not afford to pay the usual tuition fee, Kivie became enraged. He called the rabbi of the congregation, cited the incident, and asked if this was its policy. The rabbi said no and assured Kivie that he would do all he could to prevent such a practice from occurring in the future. In other words, Kivie expected congregations and those belonging to them to practice justice; otherwise, so far as he was concerned, they were betraying Judaism. He did not hesitate to excoriate prominent, influential Jews if they engaged in "blockbusting." Who gave him the authority to speak in this manner? The teachings of Judaism, he said. And he added: "I have seen so much of human misery and I do not wish to see anyone become rich through someone else's suffering."

Kivie's communal interests also included the National B'nai B'rith Career and Counseling Services; for over fifteen years he served as its treasurer. On May 11, 1974, in Washington, D.C., the National Commission of the Services presented to Kivie Kaplan the annual Wilfred S. Stachenfeld Award "in grateful appreciation for his devotion and outstanding lifelong service on behalf of Jewish youths and adults."

That his communal concerns also extended to Jewish educational endeavors is attested to by the honor he received as a fellow from Brandeis University. The citation refers to his high regard for "learning and scholarship" and his "invaluable participation in the development of the university."

In like manner, Kivie gave his support to the National B'nai B'rith Hillel program and to some local Hillel units, for

he recognized that Jewish college youths are important as a resource for leadership and talent in the future. He therefore rec-
ommended to each board on which he served that young people
be added to it. More specifically, he proposed that fifteen percent of the membership of a board should comprise young
persons. His concern that youths have a voice was no act of
condescension or tokenism to calm their militant mood for, as
he emphasized, "we need men, women, youth, black and white
to confront and buck 'the power structure.' "

Young people therefore regarded Kivie as their friend
who was always eager to give them support by championing
their causes. To illustrate, on May 21, 1973, the National Federation of Temple Youth presented Emily and Kivie with the
woodcut, "Yesterday, Today, and Tomorrow," by Irving
Amen. Their communication stated: "We look forward to
working with you in years to come to improve Jewish education, increase Jewish literacy, and enhance the quality of
Jewish life."

To honor his contribution to the furtherance of the life of
Israel, Kivie received two awards. The first was presented on
October 31, 1962, as a State of Israel Bonds Scroll of Honor at
the "Men of Vision" Awards dinner. One of the signers of the
scroll was Yigal Allon, then Israel's minister of labor. The
second award was given on May 26, 1970, by Mayor Teddy
Kolleck of Jerusalem, "for notable guidance and dedicated
service as a Founding Leader in launching the Israel Bond
Program in Boston in 1951." The inscription continues: for all
that was done "to enable the State of Israel to achieve its goal of
development in peace and freedom." On the award are the lines
in Hebrew from the prophet Isaiah: "For Zion's sake will I
not hold My peace, And for Jerusalem's sake will I not rest."

"For almost forty years," Kivie said, "I have supported
the Jewish homeland, yet I feel I would not be ethical if I
would not be critical of policies that may not be just." Hence,
in November 1972, when he went to Israel, representing the
Union of American Hebrew Congregations, as a member of the
Conference of Presidents of Major American Jewish Organiza-

*Boston, Mass., 1953.*

*With son Edward, holding Kivie's certificate of life membership in NAACP, 1955.*

*With grandson, Barry Green, holding daughter Jean Green's certificate of life membership in NAACP, 1956.*

*Kivie and family, 1959.*

*Celia Kaplan, Kivie's mother, Brookline, Mass., 1954.*

*Rabbi Richard G. Hirsch, founding director of the Religious Action Center, Washington, D.C., with Emily and Kivie, in front of dedication plaque, in the Emily R. and Kivie Kaplan Building, 1962.*

*In the Emily R. and Kivie Kaplan Building.*

*At entrance to Religious Action Center. To the right of the Kaplans are Marvin Braiterman, Rabbi Richard Sternberger, and Rabbi Hirsch.*

*Kivie and Walter Stevenson, picketing at Chicago Board of Education, 1963. Kivie and Stevenson founded the NAACP Cape Cod branch.*

*Kivie and Sidney Williams, at the NAACP
54th annual convention, Chicago, 1963.
Williams was one of more than two
hundred persons who became life members
during the convention.*

*Kivie presenting copy of career brief* Opportunities in the Peace
Corps *to Glenn Ferguson at the National B'nai B'rith Career and
Counseling Services (BBCCS) Commission meeting, 1964. The
brief was written in celebration of the 25th anniversary of the
commission. The grant for the project was provided by the Kaplans.
Left to right with Kivie are B'nai B'rith leaders: Harry Shectman,
Ferguson, Milton Berger, Esq., and Dr. S. Norman Feingold.*

*Kivie and Martin
Luther King, Jr., 1968.*

*Kivie witnessing the signing of a 30th BBCCS
anniversary proclamation by Governor John A. Volpe
of Mass., 1968. Left to right with Kivie are B'nai
B'rith leaders: Dr. Feingold, Eli Richman, and Kayla
Yampolsky.*

*NAACP annual fellowship dinner, 1968. Left to right with Kivie are Roy Wilkins, Sammy Davis, Jr., Charles Evers, and Father James E. Groppi.*

*Kivie and Bayard Rustin, recipients of the 1972 Amistad Award which recognizes outstanding individual contributions in the field of human relations. Left to right with Kivie are Rustin, Dr. C. Vann Woodward, and Dr. Charles Wesley.*

*Dedication ceremonies of the Ralph Bunche School, Long Island, N.Y., 1972. With the Kaplans is Mrs. Ralph Bunche.*

*David Ben-Gurion, at the Conference of Presidents of Major American Jewish Organizations, Jerusalem, Israel, 1972. Kivie attended as a delegate from the UAHC.*

*Shneur Zalman Shazar greets Kivie, at Conference of Presidents.*

*Kivie and Golda Meir, at a reception following Conference of Presidents.*

*Kivie conferring with Yigal Allon, at Conference of Presidents.*

*Kivie with Abba Eban and Mrs. Eban, at Conference of Presidents.*

*Kivie, at BBCCS annual meeting, Washington, D.C., 1972, at which time he was reelected treasurer. Left to right with Kivie are other commission officers: Mrs. Harold L. Blum, David M. Blumberg, Irving Rubinstein, Sr., Dr. Feingold, and Dr. Samuel E. Binstock.*

tions, he posed the question to Israeli leaders: "Why is it that better housing is provided to Jews just coming from the Soviet Union, whereas the Moroccan and Yemenite Jews, living here in Israel for twenty-five years, have substandard housing?" The answer given him was: "We need people, and the only way we can get the Russian Jews to come to Israel is by giving them better housing." When urged to elaborate what then followed, Kivie replied, "I made my point." Then he was silent.

Furthermore, Kivie was also disturbed that Conservative and Reform Jews "are cataloged as second-class citizens" in that they have no official status or recognition in Israel today. He wanted more than toleration: "There should be equality for all religious groups. We Jews should not have a system of higher and lower rank." Kivie was not only a man of words but of action, to use his language, and he therefore worked with the American Friends of Religious Freedom in Israel, of which Horace M. Kallen was president. And when he was in Israel he attended a meeting in Haifa of the League for the Abolition of Coercion in Israel. "However," Kivie said, "we did not do much. We were asked to stop activity because survival of the state was of first importance. We agreed with this." Later Kivie asked: "Can there be security if justice is denied?" Again he resumed his efforts to change the status of Reform and Conservative Jewish bodies in Israel to a position equal to that of the Orthodox.

For Kivie justice and peace were such basic values that he thought of them constantly as they affected the security and freedom of others. These values were so much a part of his life that he said simply: "Judaism is to be observed twenty-four hours a day, so the practice of justice is full time. It is demanding."

Kivie Kaplan felt he always had to be on the alert to take up the cause of whomever is oppressed and exploited. He therefore identified himself with men, women, and children in all parts of the world who merely subsisted and because they lacked the basic necessities for a secure life. He therefore supported the strike of the United Farm Workers Union, for he regarded their struggle, under the leadership of Cesar Chavez, of paramount importance. He saw that the marginal position of the Chicanos, economically and socially, makes them easy prey to exploitation. Kivie was fully aware that those who are considered inferiors, such as the Chicanos, can be paid less for doing the most grueling, backbreaking work.

When an influential communal leader complained because there was picketing in support of the grapepickers in front of a Boston market, Kivie again spoke as one who understood how workers struggle to earn their livelihood: "The rich are not interested in the poor. The only weapon that the poor man has to protect himself is to organize, protest, and engage in an ongoing struggle against 'the power structure.' " Again, he said, "It takes 'guts' to buck 'the power structure.' "

Under the auspices of the 210 Associates, a national organization established by the Shoe, Leather, and Allied Trades, he was instrumental in organizing the 210 Charity Fund. Kivie served as president of the 210 Associates.

A report of the 210 Associates states that Kivie Kaplan "was a member of the Social Service Committee for many years where he learned first hand of the needs of the less fortunate members of the industry." Later, through the Charity Trust, which was started to support "philanthropic and educational purposes," large sums were given for "college scholarships for needy youngsters." It was Kivie's contention that no poor child should be deprived of the opportunity of going to school.

When the garbage collectors of St. Petersburg, Florida, had their strike, Kivie spoke to them. The city had hired strikebreakers and paid them more than the garbage collectors were receiving and the NAACP responded with an advertisement showing how much it was costing the city and taxpayers to hire the strikebreakers. The people of St. Petersburg, protesting to the "city fathers," made the complaint: Why should we pay more to break the strike than we do for the salaries of the workers? The strike was settled, and the garbage collectors received a salary increase.

Kivie did not dismiss the important role the economic factor plays in daily life. Again and again he saw how poverty is perpetuated by prejudice, bigotry, and the status of racial inferiority. He stressed that the very social, economic, and cultural factors that breed poverty also foster racial antagonism and militarism.

It is no exaggeration to state that among rabbis Kivie is a legendary figure. Many are the stories they tell about Kivie supporting colleagues who were in difficulty because of their convictions. When he heard that the home of a rabbi was bombed in the South during the civil rights movement, Kivie called immediately to offer his cooperation even though he did not personally know the rabbi and his family. A rabbi was not receiving an adequate salary and he approached Kivie for his counsel. Kivie remarked at once: "The congregants are willing to pay taxes but do not provide a living salary to their rabbi." Kivie was concerned that rabbis should have security, "with no noose around their necks," and urged those in the rabbinate "not to be lickspittles, to cater in order to be liked." He did not hesitate to ask: "Why is it that rabbis are not as concerned as they should be about ethical and social issues?" And his answer was: "Rather than the rabbi mold the congregation, the congregation molds him."

Kivie recognized that there is no freedom in the pulpit but admitted that there are instances when rabbis will be courageous and speak their minds on important issues. When this occurs, the rabbi should know he is not alone, that he is the spokesman for those who care. When such an instance was brought to Kivie's attention, he would always send a letter of congratulation to a rabbi who had delivered a forthright sermon and would undertake to distribute the sermon widely. On the occasion when a rabbi was reluctant to take a stand on a controversial issue, Kivie urged him not to be afraid to face the criticism that would ensue. And if Kivie were to hear that a rabbi's position was threatened, he would immediately respond and create a chain reaction through telephone calls alerting others to the danger.

At the personal invitation of President Nelson Glueck and Professor Eugene Mihaly, Kivie spent a week at the Hebrew Union College–Jewish Institute of Religion in Cincinnati in order to talk to the students and faculty about the role of the rabbi in the contemporary scene. Few men, Kivie contended, live by the principles they generally espouse; their words and deeds are not synchronized. Kivie then pondered, "What prevents people from being concerned and from taking a position?" He replied, "Not everyone practices the teachings of Judaism in his or her daily life."

He was especially eager to give encouragement and moral support to the younger rabbis. Hence, when sixteen students from HUC–JIR were arrested for picketing, Kivie sent each of them letters, books, and his well-known "Keep Smiling" cards while they were jailed.

Kivie supported the peace movement with the same ardor that he championed social justice and civil rights. He argued that funds used for war purposes, which breed destruction, misery, and sorrow, should be diverted to constructive purposes to improve the quality of human life. In 1959 he met with the Peace Committees of Moscow and Leningrad to establish friendlier relations between the United States and the Soviet Union. "I felt," Kivie said, "that the bureaucrats of Washington were exaggerating the attitudes of the Russian people toward the people of the United States." It was therefore fitting that when the Union of American Hebrew Congregations presented to Emily and Kivie on December 1, 1962 (Kislev 5, 5723), its Social Action Award, a figure of Isaiah beating a sword into a plowshare was mounted on the plaque.

Kivie was a member of the Board of Enduring Peace, with headquarters in West Haven, Connecticut. Moreover, he consistently supported conscientious objectors and draft resisters and worked closely with the Jewish Peace Fellowship, taking an active part in the establishment of its Boston group. Nor was it unusual for him to be on a picket line in the early morning hours, in winter, marching in front of an army recruiting center and calling for an end to the draft for the Vietnam War.

For Kivie the concern for peace was spurred on by a principle — to realize a world of justice and brotherhood — so basic to his own life that by means of it he gained both motivation and direction.

On July 12, 1961, Kivie Kaplan attended the meeting of the NAACP with President John F. Kennedy. The gathering took place after the Freedom Ride to Washington following the NAACP convention in Philadelphia. Kivie emphasized that among those present was Medgar Evers, field secretary of NAACP in Mississippi, who was later assassinated during the civil rights struggle in the South. Obviously, Kivie was aware that whoever engages in the fight for civil rights not only undergoes physical strain but unquestionably places his or her life in jeopardy. He has to "put it on 'the line,' " Kivie said.

Emily Kaplan and the members of his family were fully aware of the risks and dangers that threatened him in his civil rights activities, yet they did not undertake to dissuade him from involving himself in the "danger zones." They gave him their fullest cooperation for they realized that what Kivie did was part of his life and that, if they had tried to restrain or stop him, they would only be crushing his buoyant, hopeful spirit.

Kivie was not self-righteous, and he did not feel he was a martyr. He knew he was not alone in whatever he did for he found allies among blacks and whites. To be specific, Kivie showed the inscription in a book that was given to him by a courageous white journalist and novelist in the South: "For Kivie Kaplan who has concern and whose concern I admire and respect."

Monetary defeats or setbacks did not perturb Kivie Kaplan for he was continually motivated by an all-consuming goal, a vision of the future when the prophetic ideal of justice, brotherhood, and peace would become a reality. His philanthropy and good deeds, organizational and communal involvements were to him not an end or final goal but means of alleviating immediate suffering. His ultimate aim was to eradicate injustice, exploitation, misery, and bloodshed so that the victims of economic injustice and racial bias could live as free persons in the future.

When asked for his social aims in capsulated form, he said, "Power must not be abused; it is a responsibility, a privilege that should be exercised for the common good. . . . Poor people must be made secure. They need new opportunities and a new environment." And he again stressed: the poor are hampered by built-in prejudices that perpetuate our social institutions.

Yes, society must be changed, he said repeatedly. Kivie the rebel did not favor individual acts of senseless violence or terrorism but advocated organized pressure by large sectors of the people, as was carried out during the movements for civil rights and peace. All methods must therefore be used to voice disapproval of and protest against existing conditions, such as the ballot and petition; the mass meeting and the demonstration; the strike, the picket line, and the protest march. Change will be brought about as social awareness is heightened through personal involvement and study. Although change is not easy and is not automatic, Kivie Kaplan emphasized that there is no justification for policies of gradualism. "Our tempo must be quickened," he said, "for young people are weary of waiting and the poor and the oppressed are calling for changes." And change must not be delayed any more, Kivie asserted.

So day by day, Kivie Kaplan, "the Man with the Heart," social idealist, lover of his people and of all humanity, defender of the exploited, strove and worked tirelessly to attain a just society.

## 8

# The Kivie Kaplan I Knew

*Richard G. Hirsch*

\*

WHEN asked why only one man was born at the Creation, the Jewish sages responded, "So that no one would ever be able to say, 'my father is better than your father'." When asked why man was created from dust taken from the four corners of the earth, they responded, "So that no one will ever be able to say, 'the place from which I come is better than the place from which you come'." When asked why man was created with every color of dust, they replied, "So that no man would ever be able to say, 'the color of my skin is better than the color of your skin'."

More than any other person in the American Jewish community, Kivie Kaplan practiced that message. Kivie passed out thousands of ties bearing the scales of justice. On the back of each tie is a label marked "Justice, Justice — K.K." There is something symbolic about the fact that one can meet people wearing Kivie Kaplan ties all over the world — people of varying interests, politics, occupations, and faiths, but all bound together in a kind of universal Kivie Kaplan brotherhood. Kivie had become "the tie that binds" people to one another through a common concern for social justice.

What was there about Kivie which bound him to people and people to him? It was not the force of his words, for Kivie was not an intellectual who transmitted new and original ideas. Nor could it have been the overflowing generosity which he and his family bestowed on all with whom they came in contact. I have often thought that if anyone else showered friends with gifts the way the Kaplans did, the recipients would begin to feel uncomfortable and perhaps even suspicious of the motivations of the donor. But not with Kivie. For with him there was no semblance of artificiality, no trace of overbearing. Unlike so many others in his financial position, he gave not to win affection but rather to show affection.

---

RABBI RICHARD HIRSCH *is the founding director of the Religious Action Center in Washingotn, D.C. He is executive director of the World Union for Progressive Judaism in Jerusalem.*

Kivie fulfilled one of the ancient dictums of Jewish tradition, "Be as zealous to perform a minor precept as a major one." Many famous people who operate on his level and at his pace cannot be expected to be bothered with matters of minor consequence. Not Kivie. No human concern was too small for his attention. He did not stand on ceremony or demand honors in accord with his status. Ask him for a small favor — to make a phone call, to write a letter — and it would be done. Ask him a dozen questions in a letter and they would all be answered. He was almost compulsive about responding to the needs of others, and he did so without imposing his own scale of priorities.

It is a natural inclination of persons who possess money and position to seek as friends and associates persons of comparable status. Not so with Kivie. Neither the dollar sign nor social status nor political influence could purchase a ticket to friendship with him. No superficial qualifications were applied, only the most exacting criteria for friendship: integrity, sincerity, compassion, conviction, personal courage, independence, simplicity. These were the qualities Kivie most admired in others, because these were the qualities which he himself possessed in such abundance.

I remember once discussing with Kivie the phrase, "Thou shalt love thy neighbor as thyself," and pointing out that the English translation distorts the original intention of the Bible. Psychologists tell us that the number of people we love the way we do ourselves is confined generally to the closest members of our family, and the trouble with many people is that they love no one the way they love themselves. Certainly the neighbor, with whom our relationships are often marred by petty annoyances, is not a person to whom such profound affection can be expressed. Then what is the Jewish interpretation? The original Hebrew provides the true intent of the biblical phrase, *Veahavta lereacha kamocha. Veahavta —* "You should love," which is normally followed by the Hebrew word *et* the sign of the direct object, is in this instance followed by the letter *l*, which connotes action. Love is not a feeling or emotion alone but requires an act. *Lereacha* — "You shall perform a deed of love to [or for] your neighbor." *Kamocha* — "He is like you."

The Hebrew injunction does not expect the impossible — no one is expected to love his fellow the way he loves himself, but rather the true meaning is to perform deeds of love for others. Why? Because he is like you. He also is a human being with your same needs and concerns. Jewish tradition does not expect all whites to love all blacks or all Christians to love all Jews any more than it expects all whites to love all whites and all Jews to love all Jews. What it does expect is that we recognize our fellow human beings as persons and treat them as we ourselves would want to be treated.

After having listened patiently to this lengthy rabbinic explanation, Kivie said, "That's beautiful. But that's the rule I've tried to follow all along the way." And so he did. Kivie cried easily. One might tell him a story of a migrant worker whose children were wracked by malnutrition and watch the tears well up. Relate the story of a middle-aged Israeli soldier whose leg was blown off in the Golan Heights during the Yom Kippur War, or depict the scene as the army notifies a man that his son has just been killed in Sinai, and out came the handkerchief.

Kivie's love of others was rooted deeply in Jewish tradition. He was always on the lookout for additional quotations to put on the new editions of his "Keep Smiling" cards. He was proud of his Jewish heritage, and he wanted others to know about it. That is why he was the world's largest private distributor of books and articles relating social issues to Jewish tradition. Unlike many liberals of Jewish extraction who deny that their Jewishness is a factor in their social convictions, Kivie went out of his way to proclaim the contribution of the historical Jewish sensitivity to justice as the motivation for his efforts.

To go with Kivie to a local chapter meeting of the

NAACP was an exhilarating experience. At the door he was met with shrieks of joy. "Hey, Kivie, keep-em-smiling!" Youngsters, oldsters, all crowded around. He called out their names. He knew thousands of NAACP members and could tell you intimate details of their life stories. He sat on the podium, listening attentively, waiting for his turn to speak. When he was introduced, he got up, without a note, not really having planned his remarks. He just got up and started talking, and out came his down-to-earth humor, a synthesis of his Jewish upbringing and his experiences on the road for the NAACP. Out came his passionate commitment and his revulsion at discrimination. And he told it like it is to his black brothers. There was no condescension about his manner or his words. He made no effort to hide who he was. He was a white man and a Jew. And he told his predominantly black audience what it means to be a Jew, and how Jews have a sense of responsibility for one another, and why as a Jew he worked for the NAACP. His audience loved him and lived it up. They interjected words of encouragement. "Yeah, man!" "Give it to 'em, Kivie!" And Kivie, stimulated by the audience response and sense of participation, poured it on. Kivie Kaplan was the epitome of empathy. He was all human. His voluminous correspondence with persons in all walks of life was an expression of his humanity. He was concerned about people, particularly about those people who were trying to help themselves. Tell him about a group of poor blacks in a small southern town who had organized a cooperative to make handbags, and Kivie would order a couple of hundred for his friends. Tell him about a scholar who had produced an important but not very marketable book, and Kivie would purchase and distribute several hundred copies. Tell him about some organization raising money through the sale of candles and Kivie Kaplan candles would illuminate the homes of all his friends.

Kivie traveled all through the South as a roving ambassador for the NAACP. Wherever he went, he made a point of contacting the rabbi and the representatives of the Jewish community. In the 1950s and early 1960s many rabbis in the South were living under severe stress. Most of them, having come from the North, were products of an integrated society. Motivated by the social imperatives of Judaism and by the historical experience of the Jews, these rabbis understood that in a society where blacks are not equal Jews could never be free and equal. In some instances, these rabbis spoke out courageously, jeopardizing their careers and their livelihoods. In other instances, rabbis suffered in silence, wanting to speak out, wanting to act, but afraid of the potential deleterious social and economic impact on their local Jewish community.

Whenever a rabbi got into difficulty with his congregation for taking a forthright position on race relations, the first person to the rescue was Kivie Kaplan. But what was even more extraordinary, he would go to great lengths to try to understand the position of the southern rabbi who found it difficult to speak out. Kivie appreciated the awkwardness of their position, he understood the inner turmoil, he suffered with them the pangs of conscience, and because of his great empathy he had a tendency to be tolerant of their reluctance to act. He said, "If a rabbi comes to a meeting of the NAACP in a southern town, that can be a greater act of courage than for a rabbi in the North to have come to Selma to march alongside Martin Luther King." Kivie knew every rabbi in the South. He was a source of support, counsel, and comfort because he understood the wisdom of the statement in Jewish tradition, "Do not judge your fellow man until you stand in his place."

As the first director of the Religious Action Center that is housed in the Emily R. and Kivie Kaplan Building in Washington, D.C., I would often report to Emily and Kivie on our various activities. They both took special delight in knowing that the building they donated quickly became a center not only for programs of Jewish groups but for a whole host of Washington-based nonsectarian organizations. A mere

listing of the organizations housed in the Religious Action
Center reflects the scope of its social concerns. At one time
or another the following organizations considered the Emily R.
and Kivie Kaplan Building their home: the Leadership Conference on Civil Rights (the coordinating agency of more
than a hundred groups responsible for the passage of all
the major civil rights bills of the 1960s); the National
Council on Agricultural Life and Labor (devoted to
improving the plight of farm laborers); the Citizens Crusade against Poverty (the coordinating agency of hundreds of groups organized by Walter Reuther as the national
citizen participation organization to combat poverty); the
National Association of Intergroup Relations Officials; the
United Negro College Fund; and other groups concerned with
such varied matters as welfare rights, home rule for the city
of Washington, civil liberties, and foreign affairs.

When the Emily R. and Kivie Kaplan Building was dedicated, an ark containing the Torah given to President Kennedy by the Union of American Hebrew Congregations at
its 1961 convention was placed in the entrance lobby. Adjacent
to it is a plaque dedicated to the Kaplans. Past the Torah and
the plaque have walked some of the major political figures of
our time, and in the conference room of the center have been
decided some of the most formative civil rights and social
welfare legislation of the 1960s and 1970s.

Kivie always welcomed the association of Judaism and
Jews with current issues, even when there was no direct
Jewish stake involved. Kivie roared at the following incident.
We received a call from a national organization which was
about to hold a highly publicized public hearing on the problems of migrant workers. The person responsible for the hearings stated, "We have decided to ask not only experts to
testify but also migrant workers themselves. We have called
the National Council of Churches to send a Protestant migrant
worker and the United States Catholic Conference to send a
Catholic migrant worker. Would you please send us a Jewish

migrant worker." After days of searching in vain, I had to report back that we could not find a Jewish migrant worker, but I asked for permission to testify myself, on grounds that as Jews we had a position and a concern — and besides, with all my peregrinations, I was the closest thing we could find to a wandering Jew.

In August 1963 the March on Washington took place. In retrospect the march has taken on the aura of respectability, but, at the time Martin Luther King, Jr., first announced it, many people, even civil rights proponents, were opposed or hesitant. There was considerable concern that the impact would be counterproductive for civil rights legislation. There was a possibility of violence, and many were opposed in principle to a situation in which they might have to engage in civil disobedience. We in the ranks of Reform Judaism consulted with our key leadership, including Kivie Kaplan, and decided that the situation called for wholehearted and active participation. We issued a call to all Jews to participate and to use the Religious Action Center as the Jewish headquarters. Thousands of Jews came from all over the country. We prepared banners in Hebrew with such biblical quotations as "Proclaim liberty throughout the land to all the inhabitants thereof," "Justice, justice shalt thou pursue," "Have we not all one father?" The first person to arrive at the center on the morning of the march was Kivie, accompanied by many of the prominent black leaders, including his friend Whitney Young of the National Urban League. Many of them picked up our banners, and one of the highlights of the television and newspaper coverage of the march was the sight of black leaders, as well as Catholic priests and nuns, marching under the Hebrew signs.

The night before the march we invited a hundred of the Jewish leaders to our home for a backyard barbecue. All the people there were avowed civil rights supporters. During the evening Kivie met a Washingtonian who proclaimed himself an ardent civil rights worker and a Kaplan admirer. Kivie sidled up to me and whispered, "This guy sounds great. Can he afford to take out a life membership in the NAACP?" I nodded in the affirmative. Kivie hit him with the pitch right then and there. The man mumbled something about sending the literature. Kivie sent several communications, but to no avail. For years thereafter Kivie would remind me of the incident with "How's your great 'liberal' Washington friend?"

Kivie could not tolerate hypocrisy or sham. He knew the difference between a profession of concern and the deed itself. In a way, he symbolized a vital turning point in the history of social action in Reform Judaism. From its inception Reform Judaism stressed the social justice dimension of Jewish tradition. In the early days of organized labor, Reform rabbis stood on picket lines to fight for the rights of labor. But it has only been in recent years that Reform Jewish laypersons have come to recognize that not only the rabbis but all Jews are obliged to implement the social imperatives of their faith. The establishment of the Religious Action Center in 1961, together with the activation of the Commission on Social Action of Reform Judaism in the late 1950s, offered effective instruments for participation in the political process.

Many so-called religionists despair of worldly affairs, or are afraid of being contaminated by political enterprises, and turn for solace to a superficial religious expression which offers distraction from the difficult realities of life. Actually, the political process is no more than the instrument by which men govern themselves. Politics is the means by which men strive to improve their lot and perfect their society. Politics will ultimately determine whether the nations of the world will learn to live together in peace or whether they will destroy one another in nuclear warfare.

The overall social, moral, and political environment is a formative influence in the life of every person. Judaism has long understood what social scientists have only recently discovered — that human beings tend to rationalize their behavior, that men generally find it easier to preach what they practice than to practice what they preach. If, therefore, the major task of religion is to shape the values of individual adherents, then one of the prime means of affecting character is to affect the character of the human environment. The Religious Action Center was established to serve as an agency for helping to change the environment through education and social action.

On the plaque establishing the center in honor of the Kaplans is written the biblical phrase, "The righteous shall live by his faith." Kivie Kaplan assuredly did that, and in so doing has instilled faith in all who knew and loved him.

# 9

## Kivie Kaplan
and the NAACP

*Roy Wilkins*

\*

KIVIE Kaplan came to the top leadership level of the National Association for the Advancement of Colored People in 1954. In 1966 he was elected its national president. In the years between, he built a solid base from which he projected his belief in the right of all persons to be treated alike, with equal access to opportunity and judged on ability alone. These are the ideals of the NAACP, and he thus was perfectly at home as a board member, officer, and just plain member. He retired from business activity, but the rules that he used in business, the relationship to people, the common sense, and the belief that the ordinary man has infinite capacity to help solve his own problems he brought from his Boston business to the NAACP.

When he started his partnership with the NAACP he chose to concentrate on its life membership program. At that time there were only 221 life members, and many of them had not paid the $500 fee in full. At the end of 1973, there were 11,877 fully paid life members and 44,208 paying on their memberships. Life members on the part of clubs, churches, unions, fraternal societies, sororities and fraternities, as well as individuals, give a depth and a scope to the NAACP that is approached by no other organization. And the center, the motivating force, was Kivie Kaplan.

Coming out of the Boston branch, to which he had belonged for many years, Kivie Kaplan burst into the heart of the national structure of the NAACP with his own kind of dream. He had his priorities, and only he could set them in focus and press them to fulfillment. As a humanist, his main goal was to help insure that all citizens received equal protection under the Constitution. His was a quest for the universal dignity of all mankind. No one should be denied his or her rights because of skin color, ethnic background, or religion. A person, he knew, was as good as his heritage.

ROY WILKINS *is executive director of the National Association for the Advancement of Colored People.*

And the heritage of us all was the universal womb from which all humans are born. He held no doubt that all men are created equal. Such principles are imbedded in the Constitution of the United States.

But the sickness of America meant that Negroes, from the day they first set foot in America at Jamestown three-and-one-half centuries ago, were to be treated unequally. People are discriminated against because the seeds of racial and ethnic hatreds that are planted in our hearts from birth are allowed to grow and be nourished.

We hear the oft-repeated story of Kivie's reaction to the hotel sign "No dogs or Jews allowed." What really bothered him was the driver's tale about the treatment of Negroes:

His words made a great impression on me. Thousands of Jews have been killed in pogroms, but for the first time in my life I realized that here were people who were being persecuted in a different way. I felt that, as a Jew, a member of a persecuted group, I should work for other persecuted races. And when I returned home I joined the NAACP.

As a measure of his commitment to the cause, Kivie practiced what he preached. His Colonial Tanning Company, which employed more than 1,000 people in seven plants around the country and did as much as $32 million in business annually, was an equal opportunity employer from its beginnings in 1924. His New Jersey tannery was the first to employ Negroes, one of whom eventually rose to become superintendent.

Kivie's opportunity to work full time (for this is what he did despite his heavy business commitments) in the fight for human dignity finally came in April 1953, when the National Board of Directors appointed him to head a drive for NAACP life members. He was elected a board member in 1954. This new role was a fitting climax to his five-year effort inside the Boston branch to get the NAACP to develop the life membership program as a fundraising project.

No idea wins acceptance before the appropriate time. The NAACP received its first life members in 1927, but the life membership program was all but neglected as the association concentrated its efforts on increasing its numerical strength, which since the early years has been its backbone. This approach to developing clout in Congress, state legislatures, and city governmental chambers made sense in that lawmakers weigh their votes by the financial and numerical strength of a measure's backers. Furthermore, the measure of a person's commitment to the civil rights struggle is oftentimes his NAACP membership card.

By 1953, the NAACP had 240,000 members, and a great many additional Americans gave their active and moral support to the movement. Such expressed support was crucial. For it meant that the black community was awakening to the fight against the physical and psychological evils of segregation and discrimination that had pervaded the land like a malignancy. This support, furthermore, was being expressed at a most critical time in the lives of Negro Americans. As the decade dawned, we were poised to accelerate the drive to overturn the legal underpinnings of the "separate-but-equal" doctrine of the land. This doctrine tragically had been given the august sanction of the US Supreme Court in its infamous 1896 Plessy v. Ferguson decision.

Membership, of course, also provided operating funds for our general budget, for underwriting most staff salaries and other basic costs such as rent, lights, and telephone. The minimum annual dues which started at $2, and a fledgling life membership program, provided us with a general fund income of $391,033 in 1953.

Another prime income source was the Legal Defense and Educational Fund, which was created in 1939 as a separate corporation and received tax-exempt authorization in 1940. But as a result of threats that the Internal Revenue Service would rescind the tax-exempt status because of our vigorous activities in other fields, notably political activity, we totally divorced the legalistic NAACP Legal Defense Fund from the NAACP in 1957.

Nevertheless in 1964 IRS regulation permitted the establishment of the NAACP Special Contributions Fund. Despite the solid support that we were receiving in the 1950s, our income was barely adequate to meet our normal expenses. Thus, in order to expand the militant drive against segregation, we had to seek new funding sources.

Shortly after I joined the national staff in 1931, the NAACP shifted from its earlier posture of principally defense to one of planned assault. Our previous concerns had been largely those of defending and protecting black Americans from the brutal waves of lynchings and other forms of savagery. No other act so expressed the baseness of the American racist psyche as those heinous crimes. No other form of abuse meted out against the descendants of the former African slaves was as cruel in its intensity.

Consequently, Walter White, upon being appointed assistant secretary of the NAACP in 1918, set out to establish his record as the greatest antilynching crusader of the century by launching an unparalleled drive to end this bestial crime. He began his investigations by touring the South. In addition to being endowed with the will and fortitude needed to pursue his goal to fulfillment, he had certain physical features that were crucial to success and survival. His light complexion and blue eyes enabled him to "pass" as a white man and thus opened up doors that would normally have been closed to a more easily identifiable black man. Thus he often conducted investigations into lynchings by visiting the actual scenes of the crimes, speaking with the lynchers themselves and painstakingly collecting the cruel details of the murders. In all, he personally investigated forty-one lynchings and eight major anti-Negro riots.

His classic work, *Rope and Faggot*, was published in 1930, a year before he was named to head the NAACP. Here Walter gives us an exhaustive study of the numbers, places, and methods of lynchings and, more importantly, the motivating factors behind them — economic, racial, religious, sexual, political, and journalistic.

His antilynching crusades further included a novel, speeches, numerous magazine articles, and an antilynching art show at one of New York's most important galleries. He also hounded every US president and every session of Congress with demands for a federal antilynching law. Although no such law was ever passed, his crusade was so unrelenting and effective that the practice of lynching finally vanished from the American scene by the time Kivie was elected to the NAACP's National Board of Directors in 1954.

An earlier study published by the NAACP, *Thirty Years of Lynching in the United States*, the first in the history of the crime, showed that, between 1889 and 1918, 3,224 persons were killed by lynch mobs. The study explained that "702 white persons and 2,522 Negroes have been victims. Of the whites lynched, 691 have been men and 11 women; of the colored, 2,472 were men and 50 were women. For the whole period, 78.2 per cent of the victims were Negroes and 21.8 per cent white persons."

In *Rope and Faggot*, Walter White likens a lynch mob to Pavlov's dog. Both mob and dog are conditioned to react automatically to certain stimuli. In the case of the white mob, the stimulus was most often a rumor that a Negro had somehow offended a white person. Says Walter:

> Generation after generation of southern whites have been handicapped and stunted in their mental and moral growth by such a situation. They have had it constantly dinned into their ears from pulpit to press, in the home and school and on the street, that Negroes are given to sex crimes, that only lynching can protect white women, that unmentionably horrible deeds can be prevented only through the use of extreme brutality. Added to this is the belief that any white man, no matter how inept, criminal, or depraved, is infinitely superior to the "best Negro who ever lived." It is a well-known fact that any idea, no matter how unsound, if

repeated often enough, and in a sufficiently assured manner, is eventually adopted by the mob as its own. One can estimate the long and difficult climb the southern white child, living in an atmosphere where dissenting opinion is ruthlessly suppressed, must make to attain even a reasonably intelligent attitude towards lynching and the Negro.

The Negro American's physical and mental suffering was as immeasurable as that endured by people living in eastern Europe during what has been called the Jewish "dark ages," and which found its horrifying resurgence with Hitler's pogroms. Similar threads in our history provide an unavoidable goal — namely, the obliteration of racial, ethnic, and religious discrimination from the soul of this land. From its founding in 1909, inspired by William English Walling's magazine article on the 1908 Springfield, Illinois, race riot, the NAACP has embodied this common goal which is held by both Negroes and Jews and all freedom-loving people. The expressed purpose of its black and white founders was to wipe out the crime of lynching and, by extension, the injustices of racism and bigotry. Through the painfully slow process of education, publicity, and appeals to our moral heritage, the NAACP aroused the conscience of the nation to the bestiality of lynching, a crime which was as dehumanizing to the perpetrators as it was cruel to its victims.

By the mid-1930s, the tide had turned. The number of mob murders had decreased, although the depravity of each act was intensified beyond mere killing to include ritual torture and dismemberment. The time being ripe for a change of strategy, we advanced our stance from one of defense to that of attack.

The year 1935 was a particularly important landmark for the NAACP. While we sadly watched the Costigan-Wagner antilynching bill succumb to a Senate filibuster, we rejoiced at our first major victory in the Baltimore City Court, involving a young black Amherst College graduate who had been refused admission to the University of Maryland Law School.

Predictably, the university drew on the commonly held bogey-man theory that a white woman would not be safe with a black man in the classroom. But the court ordered the university to admit Donald Murray if he were qualified. Murray went on to graduate and was presented his diploma by Maryland's Governor Herbert R. O'Connor. This case marked our changed emphasis to an all-out legal offensive against the fundamental basis of discrimination in education.

Upon this base, we steadily built precedents and victories that in turn became the foundation for our confident, all-out attack against the "separate-but-equal" doctrine. Under the wise guidance of Special Counsel Thurgood Marshall, whom President Johnson appointed to the Supreme Court in 1967, we built up our case bit by bit. Each victory in the courts during these years encouraged us a little more. Enheartened by the Supreme Court's decision invalidating segregation in state-supported professional and graduate schools, we pressed our well-planned campaign to overturn racial separation at its roots — in elementary and secondary schools. The drive for "equality under law" was launched in 1951 and included challenges against discrimination in several school districts. The following year, the five precedent-setting cases reached the Supreme Court. These cases involved challenges in Topeka, Kansas; Wilmington, Delaware; Prince Edward County, Virginia; Clarendon County, South Carolina; and Washington, D.C. The Supreme Court handed down its decision on May 17, 1954, upholding the right of Negroes to equal protection under the law.

The emotional and psychological pressures were great. On another front, Thurgood responded to complaints from black GIs who were fighting for their country in segregated units in the Far East. He personally visited Korea, where the men were stationed, and investigated the deplorable discriminatory practices to which they were subjected. He conferred with the soldiers and top-level Army personnel, including General of the Army Douglas MacArthur, in Japan and

Korea. He acted as counsel in several court-martial cases. At home we also won court cases that upheld the right to vote and smashed the popular housing covenants. This was a glorious march forward, and our successes in defending the rights of the downtrodden had earned us the unchallenged reputation of leader in the fight for civil rights.

This monumental march forward could not have been done on the mere strength of our numbers. With each dramatic victory, our membership dues were barely adequate to meet our general needs in time of less stress and activity. How much more inadequate was this revenue now that we were about to launch one of the most eventful eras in the history of the republic. To meet the new challenge, our then chairman of the national board, Dr. Channing H. Tobias, dramatically launched the Fight for Freedom Fund campaign in 1953 at the annual convention in St. Louis and set a yearly goal of $1 million. We set forth to eliminate all state-imposed racial discrimination and segregation by 1963, the centennial of Lincoln's Emancipation Proclamation.

An untapped source of funding at this time was the NAACP life membership program, which was created in 1910 to provide a reserve fund for our work. But until Kivie Kaplan was named to head it, the program was our proverbial stepchild. The general feeling was that few persons would be willing to contribute the seemingly high sum of $500 for a lifetime commitment to the cause. Consequently, only 221 life members had been enrolled by 1953, and a mere 88 were fully paid.

Convinced that we were not fully utilizing a most valuable resource, Kivie Kaplan in 1953 persuaded the Board of Directors to begin strengthening the program. The board therefore created a Life Membership Committee to coordinate the drive and appointed as cochairmen Kivie and Dr. Benjamin Mays, then president of Morehouse College in Atlanta. The following year Kivie was elected to his first term on the National Board of Directors. He brought his superb business skills and immense store of energy to the new challenge. He immediately set about revolutionizing the program and developed it to the point where we today have more than 53,000 life members.

His sincerity, oneness of purpose, and determination were qualities that quickly won him the title of "supersalesman." He never asked of others what he himself was afraid to do. Consequently, he consistently led each year in the number of life memberships brought in by individuals.

At the end of the first full year of the campaign in 1954, the association had gained 465 fully paid and subscribing life members. By November 26, 1957, Kivie was so elated at the success of the campaign that he wrote to thank one of the original members of the Life Membership Committee, Dr. Harry Emerson Fosdick, for his service: "Since the inception of the life membership program, more than eight hundred paid-in-full members have enlisted. At the present, there are more than two thousand individuals, churches, and organizations paying on a life membership in the NAACP."

By the following spring, the effort to popularize the program was extended. Branches and state units were encouraged to organize life membership committees, and the Kivie Kaplan Award was established to spur competition. Memos from a national coordinator reminded local branches that their treasuries received two-fifths of every life membership contribution. Churches, fraternities, sororities, civic and social clubs, and union locals were deemed excellent life membership targets. A junior life membership, which was created in 1957 to enroll children under thirteen years of age for $100, was also pressed. Kivie encouraged life membership committees around the nation to sell junior life member plaques as excellent gifts for birthdays, graduations, Christmas, or as "an expression of love at any time." "Build your local treasury with life membership funds" became the rallying cry.

Also catching on were the life membership luncheons and dinners. These events became very successful. For our golden anniversary in 1959, the "Year of Jubilee," Kivie skill-fully capitalized on the excitement of the historic period and organized a committee of fifty persons who agreed to raise $5,000 each. Thirty-three of this committee consequently turned to life memberships as a means of fund raising and gained 135 enrollees during the year. Kivie, of course, was one of the handful of persons who met the $5,000 goal. A life membership workshop was started that year to teach the finer points of gaining enrollees. In 1959, the year of the association's golden anniversary, we began publishing the *Honor Guard Booklet* with the names of all fully paid and subscribing life members.

Another example of Kivie's personal appeal could be seen in his letter to Kenneth Guscott, Boston branch president:

On July 14, I was down to the airport at Oak Bluffs to meet somebody, and this woman stopped me and asked me if I was Kivie Kaplan, and I told her I was.

. . . I told her about the life membership programs, and she told me that she would ask her husband to take one out and I would hear from her. . . .

Today I received a letter from her . . . with her check for $50 . . . [as] first payment on his life membership. You can imagine how happy this made me feel.

To Miss Evelyn Lee, whom he met on a plane, he wrote:

Thanks also for your willingness to make an investment in freedom and take out a life membership in the NAACP which is actually only 15¢ a day, $1 a week or $50 a year for ten years and you can fill out the blank and send your check along to me and I am hopeful that you may be able to get others, white and black, to do the same.

In a letter to Alfred Handy of Jackson, Mississippi, he wrote:

Thanks for your willingness to make an investment in free-dom by taking out a life membership in the NAACP. I don't have to sell you on it—I know from the talk that I had with you that you are with us, not only 100 per cent but 1,000 per cent, and I am hoping that in addition to your life membership you will get others to take some out.

He wrote to Dr. John A. Morsell, assistant executive director of the NAACP, to report that he had pursued Julian Bond, Georgia state representative, with whom he had participated on a program in Philadelphia, to take out a life membership:

I am happy that I was able to get Julian on the team with a $500 check. I hope that he will continue to grow stronger for us and on the team because we need good guys like him who believe.

In another letter to John he reported:

I thought that you and Roy would be interested in these editorials of Mr. Donald Trageser, general manager WEEI Radio and vice-president CBS Radio Division. I have been in touch with him for a few years and he finally got me in there one day for lunch, and, when I asked him about a life membership, he never heard about it, and he gave me a personal check for $500.

In all his years of approaching people for life memberships, Kivie could recall only one clear failure, and with some poignancy. This memorable moment occurred while he was conducting a tour of the South in the summer of 1964 as a member of an NAACP team testing compliance with the recently passed Civil Rights Act. Espying a well-dressed man at the entrance of a hotel in Gulfport, Mississippi, Kivie handed him one of his personalized "Keep Smiling" cards and suggested that he might want to purchase a life membership. Kivie reported:

He put both his hands into his hip pockets – I thought – but, when I looked closer, I saw that his hands were resting on the butts of two guns, one on each side. Then, opening his coat, he displayed a sheriff's badge pinned to his shirt and started saying words that I would never ever repeat or want to put in print. In all my years I don't think I have ever moved away from anyone so fast.

Thus, whether it was on a plane, at home, or abroad, Kivie's appeal for life members was as certain as his ubiquitous "Keep Smiling" cards. The cause of human justice was to him as dear as the survival of Israel and, I think it is safe to say, both were coequal in his order of universal priorities. None of his friends, therefore, escaped his dunning for support of the NAACP. Every member of his family, fifty-eight in all — children, grandchildren, cousins, and in-laws — is a life member of NAACP. The full extent of this devotion can only be realized when one remembers that a life membership is not tax-deductible, since it goes into our general fund; only contributions to the NAACP Special Contribution Fund afford tax write-offs.

In Kivie Kaplan's eyes, people were not black or white, Jew or Gentile, but mortals deserving of the self-evident truth that all of us are created equal. As a means of successfully waging the fight for equal justice, therefore, he saw as indispensable the need for a financially strong institution such as the NAACP. He faithfully adhered to the principle of its founders that the NAACP is neither a white nor a black organization. It is an institution dedicated to securing equal justice for all people. The fact that racial injustice against black people claims the overwhelming portion of the NAACP's resources was incidental to Kivie's way of thinking. This is a mere historical coincidence that, to be fully understood, must be measured against man's inhumanity to man since time immemorial.

His endless search for life memberships often led him to employ the tactics of a Baptist preacher at the end of a dinner or luncheon and spend the next hour or so imploring and cajoling his audience for new subscriptions. He was an expert at such scientific techniques as picking through the pages of magazines like *Ebony* and *Jet* in quest of likely prospects. A most excellent source of life members, he believed, should be *Ebony* magazine's list of one-hundred outstanding black people, many of whom are certainly not life members.

He passed along this bit of wisdom to the current director of the NAACP Life Membership Division, Edward B. Muse, and explained that a corps of volunteer solicitors should be created. He felt that starting in a small way would give the program room to grow.

An idea of the esteem with which Kivie was held by the staff of the NAACP may be understood by the expressions of the veteran Clarence M. Mitchell, Jr., director of the Washington bureau, and the then chairman of the National Board of Directors, Bishop Stephen Gill Spottswood.

Mr. Mitchell declared:

I met him when he first came on the Board and I must confess that I had a sneaky feeling that he was giving more of his time to the NAACP than to his business. He would have had to be two men to do otherwise.

He never hesitated to get people, high and low, to join. One of his techniques was to explain the payment plan. He got [Massachusetts Governor] John Volpe to join. I am sure he got contributions from Ted Kennedy.

He had an extensive interest in human rights and values. He donated the building in which the Leadership Conference has offices. Kivie was warm and friendly. I have great admiration for him, because he was the kind of person who always had his feet on the ground with race relations.

He participated in all the marches and demonstrations, always going right down at the scene. He was at the Medgar Evers funeral. He took speaking engagements in the South. He was always ready to lend a helping hand. Whenever I asked him to see a few congressmen and senators he would do so.

During the NAACP convention in 1966 in Los Angeles, he was attacked by a Nazi who ran upon the platform and cried, "Kivie Kaplan, you communist." The man was prevented from reaching Kivie. But, even in the face of physical danger, Kivie was very calm, not unnerved at all by that incident. Someone else might have said, "I'd better get out," but that didn't slow him down any.

One of his greatest assets was persistence. . . . Once people fell within his sight as possible life members, they hardly escaped.

He came through the black upheaval with principles on integration intact because he had a deeply ingrained sense of human rights. If you start with the premise that a man is entitled to equality, freedom, and justice, even if some of the victims start acting as oppressors themselves, your principles don't change.

Another notable quality about Kivie Kaplan is that his convictions on human dignity did not change to suit the times. To cite the role of the NAACP in any situation is to cite the role of Kivie.

Bishop Spottswood said of him:

I was initially sorry when he was elected president, because I felt he wouldn't give enough time to the life membership campaign — although I was instrumental in getting him elected. He was a savior of the NAACP in the fifties.

At the time Kivie Kaplan was elected, it was violently stated at a small caucus that we don't need any white people to head this organization.

But Kivie Kaplan was not elected because we felt we needed a balance of parts. We did not want to imitate white people who ignore Negro membership when selections are at hand.

Through the years the titular head of the NAACP has been white. After John R. Shillady resigned, the spokesman for the organization has always been black. The national NAACP policy is set by the resolutions of the delegates at our annual convention. We feel a white titular head is a good thing for an interracial body. We said by Kivie Kaplan's election that we don't need an all-black organization.

The NAACP is not a black association, nor is it a white association. It is an American association.

Kivie Kaplan was a composite man, religiously. He belonged to an Orthodox synagogue, a Reform temple, and the United Church of Christ. At Martha's Vineyard, he also accepted membership in the Congregational Church, where he was an officer.

Unlike many white liberals, Kivie Kaplan came through the period of black militancy unscathed and without bitterness.

I would attribute that to his sincerity and dedication to the cause. There has never been a man more dedicated to the NAACP than Kivie.

# 10

# Kivie and Reform's Social Action

*Albert Vorspan*

*

K IVIE KAPLAN was unique, in both his life and his death. His death, in May of 1975, was consistent with his life. He died with his boots on, en route from a meeting in Washington to a meeting in New York City. For months, Kivie had been ailing. After one of his serious heart failures, his doctor had implanted a pacemaker and urged Kivie to take it easy. Kivie always promised to slow down, but — unconsciously — he knew he would not be Kivie if he became a pale face in the window, looking out on life. Kivie preferred to live actively and intensely, right to the end, to burn out rather than rust out. James Hicks, wrote in the *Amsterdam News* right after Kivie's death:

He had some speaking engagements in Safety Harbor, Florida, and while speaking on one engagement he had a run in with some Nazis and this took a lot out of him. But he went on from there to St. Petersburg where he and 72-year-old Probyn Thompson worked up a dinner for 103 people and persuaded 58 of them to buy NAACP life memberships.

He quoted from a letter he received from Kivie, describing his winter "vacation":

We left Safety Harbor on March 12 and drove 256 miles from there to Thomasville, Ga., where I spoke with 10 of the officers and NAACP Board for dinner and then I spoke that evening at a mass meeting. The next morning we drove 157 miles to Macon in time to speak for the Ministers luncheon and we were there for three days for the Region Five convention. Then on to Chapel Hill Branch in North Carolina and so on until we went home (to Boston) on March 26 when we had two Passover Seders, the 26th and 27th.

You could see Kivie's life mirrored at his funeral. Almost 1,000 people filled the sanctuary in Temple Israel, Boston — mostly Jews and blacks. Kivie was the bridge between Jews

---

ALBERT VORSPAN *is vice-president of the Union of American Hebrew Congregations and director of the Commission on Social Action of Reform Judaism.*

and blacks during his life, and even at his death. Senator Edward Brooke, mourning quietly in the pew, told his neighbor that there was no way he could ever have become a United States senator if there were no Kivie Kaplan. Kivie touched more people, the ordinary and the mighty, than anybody I ever met. You could see the emotion on the faces, the personal pain, the immensity of the loss in the synagogue. At the funeral, people mentioned gift packages and books they had received from Kivie only days before. I had my usual daily correspondence from Kivie on my desk the day he died. Kivie died in full swing, as he would have wanted to. To the end, he devoted his life to his twin concerns — the fight for human equality and the welfare of the Jewish people. His dream was of renewed black-Jewish collaboration in the great task of social justice. There was no American with greater contacts and esteem in both groups. Dozens of newspapers editorialized on the meaning of his life; the *Boston Globe* headed its editorial "Keep Smiling, Kivie Kaplan." In his life and in his death, he symbolized the cooperation of blacks and Jews, earning the opprobrium of bigots in both groups, the condescension of the few, and the deep admiration of countless people in numberless towns and cities. Kivie Kaplan's death could be the end of an era, for who is there in this entire land who has earned the trust of so many people in both races? Or — if we remember him rightly, if we truly honor his memory — it could be an inspiration for a new beginning.

When Kivie died, the Union of American Hebrew Congregations in New York City placed Kivie's picture in its Fifth Avenue window with an appropriate memorial. That day, a black man stopped in front of the window, looked at the memorial, took a "Keep Smiling" card out of his wallet, and — lovingly — tucked it in the window.

Will there ever again be a Jewish president of the NAACP? Maybe not; maybe there shouldn't be. But, with Kivie, it was not a historical anachronism. He did more for the NAACP than any other layperson in the land. He kept it afloat; he poured himself into its work. He safeguarded its future. Virtually every other civil rights organization has either evanesced or lost its mooring — sometimes drastically. The NAACP has stood like a watchman at the gate, true to its commitment to an integrated society. Without Kivie's endless work, the NAACP's endurance would have been doubtful and America would be poorer.

Kivie Kaplan felt himself personally involved in the fight against segregation and injustice wherever it erupted, whoever the victim. His private correspondence — separate from and apparently of higher priority than his business correspondence — ran to something like 500 letters a week.

In contrast to the rhetorical liberals who love people in the abstract and are bored by them individually, Kivie had little patience with theories of human relations but liked people, individually and collectively. He was a walking CARE package whose personal warmth was a joy to his friends and an inspiration for strangers caught up in the fearful storms of struggle for a better world.

When in the late fifties Rabbi William Silverman became the target of heavy community pressure and threats as a result of his antisegregation statements in Nashville, Kivie picked up the phone in Boston and called him. The fact that he had never before met the rabbi was quite beside the point. He offered his warm support and encouragement and, when the going got rough for the rabbi's wife and kids, Kivie invited them to fly up to Boston to be his guests for a few days. Exceptional? Standard operating procedure for Kivie Kaplan, whose home was a lighthouse for college students, black youngsters, beleaguered clergymen, harried editors, all those who got tossed about.

If you called on Kivie in his home near Boston, it was probably bustling with people. A variety of social justice devotees, laypersons and professionals, were no doubt scattered about the place like the Sunday newspapers. Laughing joyously, Kivie presided over the bedlam like a happy warrior, passing out libations and pamplets with evenhanded impartiality. Pretty soon, Kivie showed you an immense closet in which you found mountains of books and periodicals which he showered on his friends. There was another closet from which packages were assembled (tea, cookies, jams, toys, address books) for frequent mailings to the long and growing list of Kaplan friends (many of whom he had still to meet), including always a set of "Keep Smiling" cards in a dozen languages. (Kivie made a sensation when he and Emily visited Russia and showered these cards . . . in Russian . . . on everyone they met.)

Kivie Kaplan was more than a colorful, fascinating person, more than a generous institution, more than a name of a building and an inspiration for social action. He was a rare person — whose fate was to care, really care, in an age when caring had become deeply suspect, if not oddball. And he was more than just an offbeat individual. He was a symbol of Jewish commitment to human equality and of how much good one person, if he cared enough, could spread in a society in one lifetime. He was a symbol, at a time of black-Jewish tension, of how a person could stand with one foot in the black community (NAACP) and his other foot in the Jewish community (UAHC, synagogues, Jewish philanthropies, Israel, etc.) and be a whole person, proudly erect, integrated in his own values, without falling on his face.

And just as Kivie became both a legend and a symbol of the NAACP's determined insistence upon integration rather than separatism, so was Kivie Kaplan a symbol of Reform Judaism's commitment to social justice.

Kivie Kaplan was elected in 1958 to the National Commission on Social Action of Reform Judaism, the joint instrumentality of the UAHC and the Central Conference of American Rabbis. He joined his rabbi, Roland Gittelsohn (who had sponsored his nomination), and thirty other rabbis and laypersons in the work of applying the ethics of Judaism to racial injustice and other social issues in the general community. He was reelected every term thereafter. In the commission, Kivie relished the comradship of such devoted social actioniks as Irving Fain of Providence, who served for many years as chairman; I. Cyrus Gordon, attorney and long-time chairman; Joe Rauh, dynamic battler for civil liberties, justice for union members, and compassion in government policies; and many others.

Kivie also became a close associate of the staff of the commission and the UAHC, giving freely of his time and energy and funds to expand the social action program of Reform Judaism, which had originally emerged as the vision of Rabbi Maurice Eisendrath, former president of the UAHC. As the commission strove to stimulate social action committees in every Reform synagogue in America, it increasingly felt the need for the development in the nation's capital of an arm of the commission, through which the voice and positions of modern Judaism could be felt in the highest policymaking places of the federal government. Everyone acknowledged the need. But Kivie also saw the way: himself.

In 1959, at the UAHC Biennial Assembly, delegates voted overwhelmingly to accept a $100,000 gift extended by Kivie and his wife for the establishment of a Religious Action Center in Washington as an agency of the Commission on Social Action of Reform Judaism. It was pointed out by Rabbi Eisendrath, in his State of the Union message, that the center would function under the supervision of the national commission and that it would work in close harmony with the many Protestant and Catholic social action agencies with similar offices in Washington.

In the months following the 1959 General Assembly, several Reform synagogues joined together in a concerted and well-organized campaign to stop implementation of the plan for a Washington center. Even after a building was purchased in Washington as the site for the Emily R. and Kivie Kaplan Religious Action Center (an old embassy on the corner of 20th Street and Massachusetts Avenue, NW), the propaganda campaign mounted — at an increasing tempo. Opposition to the center brought together an unlikely coalition of dissidents, including some southern congregations seething at UAHC stands on racial integration; anti-Zionists who refused to swallow Reform Judaism's pro-Israel posture; and conservatives who bitterly feared "lobbying" by a religious organization and who contended that the right of individual dissent would be destroyed by a national body speaking out on political and social issues.

The administration of the UAHC, conscious of the divisions which were developing on this issue, decided to place the question on the agenda for the 1961 General Assembly in Washington. Thus the stage was set for one of the most dramatic confrontations in the occasionally stormy history of American Judaism. Few debates — excepting those over Zionism, participation in the American Jewish Conference, and the move of the UAHC from Cincinnati to New York City — generated as much emotion or were so laden with long-range and symbolic significance for the Reform Jewish movement in this country.

It was 2:00 P.M., Tuesday, November 14, 1961. The large ballroom of the Sheraton Park Hotel in Washington, D.C., was almost full. Harried ushers scrutinized the credentials of each person who sought entry to the roped-off section reserved for delegates. More than one notable, having forgotten his badge, had to hurry back to his room to retrieve it. Visitors, some coming from New York City only for this particular session, streamed into the balcony to watch the drama.

Approximately 1,300 official delegates to this Forty-sixth General Assembly of the UAHC, representing Reform synagogues throughout the United States and Canada, had registered for the convention, which had begun two days earlier. All were in their seats that Tuesday afternoon, voting cards and resolutions in their hands. The vast hall was charged with suspense.

Judge Emil N. Baar, permanent chairman of the convention, standing under a banner setting forth the convention theme of "Judaism and Democracy: Our Common Mission," strode to the podium and gaveled the session to order.

Many of the Reform Jewish leaders in the room had also attended the 1959 Biennial Assembly in Miami Beach, where the controversy had really begun. In Miami Beach the delegates had voted overwhelmingly to accept the gift of Mr. and Mrs. Kivie Kaplan for the establishment of a center for religious action as part of the program of the Commission on Social Action of Reform Judaism. Thereafter, a building had been purchased in the nation's capital, but implementation of the center had been postponed as a result of determined opposition on the part of several of the Reform synagogues which make up the UAHC.

Led by Congregation Emanu-El of New York City and the Washington Hebrew Congregation, the opposition had waged a zealous campaign for reconsideration of the entire matter at the next convention. Because of the importance of the issue, the UAHC leadership agreed to place the question once again, for full debate and action, before the 1961 General Assembly.

In the months preceding the 1961 convention, the air had been purple with charges and countercharges. It was clear that the opposition combined a variety of forces and views. Some were vehemently opposed to social action altogether, holding that the application of Jewish ethics to social issues and daily life was the duty of the individual and not of the synagogue or of the Reform Jewish movement. Some were strongly opposed to the idea of a social action center in Washington, fearing it would smack of "lobbying" and would involve Reform synagogues in "controversial" issues. Some southerners objected because of the UAHC positions on desegregation. The American Council for Judaism loosed a wild charge that the center was part of some dark trend toward "monolithic" institutions. One or two others, unconcerned with social action one way or the other, saw in the issue an opportunity to challenge the leadership and basic direction of the UAHC.

Each side was given fifty minutes to present its case. It became immediately evident that the opposition had begun to retreat from its original position. Instead of directly opposing the center or social action ("Let me emphasize that we are all *for* social action"), it concentrated on a demand for additional "safeguards" in the center's operation. Specifically, it pressed for an amendment demanding a "watchdog" advisory committee to be made up of laypersons who were not members of the Commission on Social Action. The issue then became: would such a "watchdog" committee stifle or emasculate the social action program? Supporters of the center contended it would; opposition speakers insisted it would give the congregations additional necessary protection.

Distinguished members of Reform Judaism were to be found on both sides of the controversy.

An enthusiastic message of support for the center from then US Secretary of Labor Arthur Goldberg was read to the delegates. An interesting aspect of the controversy is that Goldberg, several years earlier, had been among the first to propose the establishment of a social action center under Reform Jewish religious auspices which would work side by side with the many Protestant and Catholic social action agencies already functioning in Washington.

Even in the early stages of the debate it was evident where the sentiments of the delegates lay. The opposition was singularly unpersuasive. The vote was overwhelming — approximately 1,200 to 100. A triumphant roar of gratification echoed through the hall, almost drowning out the chairman's announcement that the amendments were defeated and the main resolution carried.

It was a dramatic moment, the climax of a memorable convention. After the smoke of battle cleared, it was manifest that all the sound and fury of the past months had been generated by a small minority. The Union of American Hebrew

Congregations, in keeping with a tradition going back to its inception in 1873, had resolved to keep faith with its commitment to social justice.

The Emily R. and Kivie Kaplan Center for Religious Action was formally dedicated in 1962.

The center has, in the stormy years of its existence, more than justified the hopes of the Kaplans and of the Reform movement. It has represented the American Jewish religious community, via the Synagogue Council of America (which is comprised of Orthodox, Conservative, and Reform branches), on national legislative issues such as antipoverty measures, welfare reform, and Soviet Jewry. In behalf of American Jewry, Rabbi Richard Hirsch, then the center's director, appeared before Congress alongside Protestant and Catholic spokesmen to express religious support for the great landmark civil rights bills of the sixties — a historic unity of the three faiths in support of concrete and controversial legislation. The center helped to mobilize the interreligious campaigns for these measures, and all objective observers listed the work of the religious community as a major force in breaking the backbone of racial segregation in the United States Congress.

In the long and desperate struggle against the Vietnam War, the Religious Action Center became a virtual peace center. When massive demonstrations of concerned citizens poured into Washington to register their anguished protests against this monstrous war (the UAHC condemned the war in 1965), the center served as the base for the many Jews — young and old — among them. Religious services, briefings, sandwiches, guidance, and medical teams were available at 2027 Massachusetts Avenue, NW; many young people also bedded down for the night at the center. More than once, tear gas attacks against peaceful protesters near Dupont Circle drove many distressed peaceful citizens into the center which, in the incredible years of the war, made the center a sanctuary and first-aid station for any who needed refuge.

In between national crises, which seemed to be the normal

rhythm of the sixties, it served also as an educational and training center in Jewish social action. Protestant, Catholic, and Jewish seminary students came there to learn the techniques of effective religious social action. National Federation of Temple Youth leaders from all parts of the country made pilgrimages to Washington where, through the center, they met congressmen, talked with Supreme Court justices and White House officials, called on the Israeli embassy, learned how to go to the Hill to express their views, got an inside look at how government functions. Jewish educators gather at the center to consider how better to relate Jewish ethics to the political and social realities of our nation and our time.

Thus, faithful to the vision of Kivie and those who sought to translate it into a program, the Religious Action Center has become a true center of Jewish social conscience. Arthur Goldberg addressed the leaders of Reform Judaism at the special dedication ceremonies on December 1, 1962. He recalled that Reform Judaism had presented a special Torah (one brought to the United States by Isaac Mayer Wise) to President Kennedy in the Rose Garden (at which time Kennedy smilingly told an associate who chided him for not wearing a hat: "Look, I'm a *Reform* Jew"). That Torah is now permanently and appropriately housed at the center. Said then Secretary of Labor Goldberg:

This center does not enshrine the Torah; it is enlightened by it. Its presence here makes clear to all who enter that the meaning of Torah is to act in His will and to follow in His path, remembering always that these are the words of a *Living* God.

This is the law, commanded unto us by Moses and the prophets. It is our heritage, we who are the congregation of Jacob. Its laws are the laws of all men. Its truths are truths for all men. No power on earth can be as frail or as forceful as the power of this Torah. It can be and it has been burned and torn, calumnied and reviled. It has survived! Acts of hatred have in no way diminished its vitality or imperative, for men know that it is these words which they must take with them as they seek to return to the Lord their God.

Show me a community in which religious leaders are willing to lead and I will show you a community that is willing to face its problems.

Show me a nation in which religious leadership stands to be counted on every important social and economic issue, and I will show you a nation that will hold its head high before all of history.

Accepting the Torah from Rabbi Eisendrath in the ceremony at the White House, President Kennedy declared:

I want to express my great satisfaction in welcoming you to the White House again and to tell you how grateful I am for your generosity. These Torahs I know have special significance for you, and particularly this one, which is so intimately associated with the founder here in the United States, one which is brought from Europe and which has been part of your life. So I am doubly appreciative to you for being willing to part with it and present it to us here today.

I think, as the rabbi said, that the significance of this ceremony is not merely a gift of an ancient document but that in a very real sense the great issue today is between, as he said, the supremacy of the moral law which is initiated, originated, and developed in the Bible and that which has special application here today.

I have never felt that we should attempt to use the great impulse towards God and towards religion, which all people feel, as an element in a cold war struggle. Rather, it is not an arm, it is the essence of the issue — not the organization of economy so much but as the supremacy of moral law and therefore the right of the individual, his rights to be protected by the state and not be at the mercy of the state.

In the Inaugural Address, which the rabbi mentioned, I said that the basic issue was that the rights the citizen enjoyed did not come from the state but rather came from the hand of God. And it is written here. And it is written in the Old and New Testaments.

So I am grateful to you, and I want you to know that in coming here today I think it symbolizes the happy relations which exist between all religious groups, and must continue to exist in this country, if we are to be worthy of our heritage.

So, Rabbi, I am grateful to you. There is no gift which could please me more — and I am delighted to welcome you to your house.

In a separate message of congratulations, the president wrote:

Congratulations upon the establishment by the Union of American Hebrew Congregations of a Religious Action Center in Washington. This is an effective answer to those who deny the responsibilities of religion for sectarian injustice. It emphasizes ethical and moral principles, which should be a part of the foundation of any religion.

I should particularly like to congratulate and offer my best wishes to Mr. and Mrs. Kaplan, whose generosity permits the construction of the building to house the Religious Action Center.

Please give my best wishes to all those attending the ceremonies surrounding this dedication.

But the difference between Kivie and other philanthropic figures was that Kivie did not just write a check and go on to other things. He invested *himself.* The professional people of the commission were not viewed by Kivie — as is the case with many other benefactors in other agencies — as mere paid help. They were his close personal friends and coworkers because Kivie also worked full time in social action. He was a tireless goad and encourager to the staff, to members of the commission, to rabbis and social action chairmen all over the country. His personal correspondence was vast. Let a rabbi be threatened by a congregation for taking a strong stand on a social issue, and Kivie would put in a call to the rabbi immediately, urging him to stand fast, telephone the CCAR to appeal to them to keep the rabbi from being pushed around, and write and/or call members of the congregation to go to bat for justice. And you didn't have to be a rabbi to win Kivie's help. If a black family took its lumps for the sin of moving into an angry all-white community, or sending their brave child into the teeth of hysterical rednecks at school, Kivie took that as a personal responsibility. Perhaps he would write them, sending them books and other gifts of encouragement. If his hectic travels for the NAACP took him into that part of the country, he'd drop in unannounced to shake their hands. If the tension in the community began to wear them down, Kivie might send them plane tickets to come up to stay with him and Emily in Chestnut Hill or Martha's Vineyard. A host of the civil rights heroes, sung and unsung, of the past twenty years were Kivie's long-time friends, including mature women who were once the scared black schoolchildren running the gauntlet in Little Rock, Arkansas.

Considering the vast responsibilities which lie on the NAACP, the significance of Kivie Kaplan's achievement is clear. When he would fly into New York, black porters would jockey for the privilege of handling his bags. They would not accept tips from him. Instead they warmly yielded to his sales pitch for added NAACP contributions. So did waiters in restaurants. In the NAACP, Kivie was not just another white friend; he was an institution. But Kivie Kaplan was more than that, too. He was out for results, not only money.

Emily and Kivie spent their summers in a pleasant old home in Martha's Vineyard. They found that the nearby beach club didn't admit Jews or blacks as members. That's all Kivie had to learn. Within a few weeks, the WASP elite in charge of the club must have wondered what had hit them. Kivie was admitted; Art Buchwald and other Jewish summer residents are now also members of the club. But just as the Yankees must have suspected in their secret fears, after the Jews would the blacks be *far* behind?

When the moguls dragged their feet on the applications of several black families, Kivie felt the time had come for more subtle moral suasion. He persuaded his immediate neighbor, himself a blueblood Yankee brahmin, to inquire at the club as to what was holding up the black applications. Inasmuch as Kivie's Yankee friend also happened to be the local tax assessor, the door flew open to a gorgeously rainbow-hued membership where a dull WASP bastion had only so recently presided.

Kivie was almost always in the midst of conflict. Many Jews baited him for being a "Negro lover" and, therefore, "traitorous to Jews." Some members of the spa in Florida which Kivie and Emily attended every winter looked at him askance, especially when his NAACP friends came to visit. On the other hand, many black militants scorned him as a "honkie" and tried at every NAACP convention to replace him with a black. Uniformed American Nazis followed him around in the last months of his life. But Kivie rarely lost his temper. "The guy who loses his cool loses the advantage," he said.

Contrary to his public image as a flaming liberal, radical, or crackpot, Kivie was a moderate Republican. His politics were close to those of his good friend, Senator Edward Brooke of Massachusetts. Kivie usually voted Republican on the presidential level, but he drew the line at Richard Nixon — and he never regretted it. "As a Republican, I am ashamed of the [Nixon] Administration's lack of understanding for the black man," he said. "Eighteen years after 1954, for an administration to want to countermand a Supreme Court decision is not just, legal, or moral."

Kivie was close to his children — two daughters and a son — and doted on his grandchildren. His faith in the future rested with the young. "Young people are wising up to racial justice," he said. "They don't have our hang-ups. Unfortunately, you have to wait for these old bigots to die before the young people come in." Kivie's rapport with young people — black, white, Jewish, or mixed — was a marvel to behold.

Kivie proudly accepted the charge that he was a "Negro lover" and said he was also a "Jew lover," but he signed no blank checks for either group. What offended his principles he blasted. Anti-Semitism angered him, whether it came from whites or blacks. There can be little doubt that his influence contributed, in no small measure, to the NAACP's unfailing opposition to racism, anti-Semitism, and Third World anti-Israel mythologies. But Kivie also condemned the tendency of many Jews to exaggerate the extent of black anti-Semitism in order to justify their own cop-out on racial justice. "Anti-Semitism among blacks, especially young blacks, is probably growing, but at no greater rate than anti-Negroism among Jews," he once said.

While in Israel representing the UAHC as part of a delegation of major Jewish organizations, Kivie was shocked to see the exaggerated perception Israeli leaders had of black anti-Semitism in the United States. Typically, he got up and told them so:

Black anti-Semitism is only a pinprick of anti-Semitism in America. White bigots are doing all within their power to keep Jews and blacks at each other's throats. Every study confirms that anti-Semitism in America is still overwhelmingly the plague of white Christians. Despite everything, blacks and Jews share the same deep need for an open and just society.

On the plane returning home from Israel with fellow delegates from every major Jewish organization, Kivie heard a rabbi murmur to his partner: "That's Kivie Kaplan; he's not for *us*. He works for the *shvartze*." He was used to such harpoons, but they only goaded him, never beached him.

Kivie was an inspiration and a goad to many, both black and white, and he became a living legend in American life. He worked for *us* all his life, and his memory will be a blessing to all who cherish justice and decency in the world.

## 11

# His Convictions
# and Courage

*Gloster B. Current*

*

He hath showed thee, O man, what *is* good; and what the Lord doth require of thee, but to do justly, and to love mercy, and to walk humbly with thy God.

Micah 6:8

K IVIE Kaplan, to me, was one of the best examples of the man who abides by the admonition of the prophet Micah.

Kivie, as he was affectionately called by all who knew him, was a man of goodness, justice, mercy, and humility. He was frank and outspoken, a man who not only believed in religion but practiced it daily. Moreover, he was tolerant and supportive of other faiths. A doer, he had little patience with those who procrastinated or whose actions revealed them to be phoneys.

Kivie would go out of his way to help not only his friends but people he did not know. His love of family was paramount. His love of humankind was a rare attribute not found in many persons today. He was devoted to Jewish causes, naturally. But his devotion to race relations was such that I doubt whether the full dimension of this contribution will ever be known or recognized.

As one who was associated with Kivie Kaplan since he became a member of the NAACP National Board, I want to recall a few events which to me illustrate his uniqueness.

The National Board meetings of the NAACP in New York were memorable to a young staff officer, for they were attended by people long revered in the struggle for human rights and dignity.

Dr. S. Ralph Harlow, professor at Smith College, also a board member, arose in one of the monthly meetings in 1953 to propose the name of his esteemed friend, Kivie Kaplan of Bos-

---

GLOSTER CURRENT *is director of branches and field administration of the NAACP.*

ton, for membership on the NAACP Board of Directors. Few had heard of the efforts of the Boston leather manufacturer in the field of race relations, but Dr. Harlow was so persuasive in extolling his virtues that the board, on recommendation of Walter White, then executive secretary, nominated Kivie Kaplan, who subsequently was elected by the membership to an at-large seat.

I shall never forget Kivie's first board meeting on February 8, 1954. Introduced by Dr. Harlow and asked to say a few words, Kivie responded with candor, calling attention to the association's life membership program. Walter White had just finished lamenting the NAACP's dire financial plight, a chronic situation.

Kivie began by indicating that the life membership program was a veritable "gold mine" and should be worked properly. Life memberships cost $500, and at the time the NAACP had fewer than 100 of them.

Looking around the room at the distinguished NAACP leaders, Kivie said that each member of the board should become a life member. Dr. Channing H. Tobias, long associated with the national YMCA and himself a veteran fund raiser, who was presiding, agreed with Kivie and on the spot appointed him as cochairman of the life membership campaign along with Dr. Benjamin Mays. From that day on, the life membership program of the association began to grow until today it numbers over 53,000.

Kivie's sales tactics often irritated some of the less affluent members of the national board. A black doctor, who was a hard-working state and local branch president, complained to Chairman Tobias at a meeting in 1955 that Kivie had no right to solicit board members for life memberships. Dr. Tobias, who was on Kivie's side 100 percent, said, "Now listen, Doctor, Kivie is working for the association. He is not working for himself. Don't you say anything derogatory of Kivie. You let him do anything he wants. If he's thinking big and wants to help us, then we, too, have got to think big."

Another side of Kivie Kaplan, not known, perhaps, was the personal interest he took in the association's employees, board members, state conference officers, and numerous branch presidents. Kivie once told me how he spent many hours getting key employees not to resign because of salary differentials with other organizations. Kivie explained to them that "the cause is the important thing." Kivie would tell them that their personal feelings were unimportant. "If anybody has a right to feel hurt," Kivie would say, "I've probably got a right to feel hurt. I am a Jew and I'm white and I've endured a lot of insults. But I believe in the cause. Judaism teaches us that all people are created equal in the eyes of God and we are not free until everybody is free. This is my way of practicing Judaism."

When my daughter was hospitalized in Virginia with suspected tuberculosis (later diagnosed as sarcadosis), she was down in spirits as anyone would be in such circumstances. Kivie sent several of his "Keep Smiling" cards and books which she in turn distributed to other patients. The nurses asked for a supply of the cards which Kivie gladly sent in large quantity.

I asked Kivie how he became inspired to pass out "Keep Smiling" cards. He told me:

Originally my son-in-law Morton Grossman's company had a card that said "Smile" and on the back it gave Grossman's lumber company's name and address. I liked the idea of the "Smile" but I didn't like the idea of the advertising, so I got a message with a thought. And then I eventually came to "Keep Smiling." I changed the message every 10,000. I'd pick up messages as I went along and then I'd print 10,000 and then, when I'd begin to run low, I'd order another 10,000 with a new message.

Kivie distributed many thousands of these messages printed in many languages throughout the world, including Japan and Russia. The Russians wanted to know if he was a missionary. Kivie answered yes. Asked with what church he was connected, Kivie said that, although he was not connected with a church, he believed in brotherhood; that all people are created equal and everybody should get along with everybody. Kivie gave the Russians ballpoint pens and books, and they, in turn, began to load the Kaplans with presents.

On one occasion Kivie's distribution of "Keep Smiling" cards almost resulted in an untoward incident. It happened in Mississippi in July 1964, during an exciting five-day automobile trip to Jackson, Canton, Meridian, Philadelphia, Gulfport, and Clarksdale, during which a team of NAACP board and staff members tested the public accommodations section of the Civil Rights Act signed by President Lyndon B. Johnson earlier that month.

At the June 25 meeting of the National Board of Directors held in conjunction with the Fifty-fifth Annual Convention of the association in Washington, D.C., the board voted to send a committee of its members and staff to Mississippi to evidence concern for the protection of civil rights in that state as well as to observe the investigation into the fate of three young civil rights workers who had disappeared around Philadelphia: James Chaney, Michael Schwerner, and Andrew Goodman.

During the convention, NAACP delegates had staged a public protest around the Department of Justice. Officials of the NAACP had conferred with the attorney general and President Johnson.

There was considerable discussion in the board meeting about the committee's trip, including necessary security measures to protect NAACP officials. The State of Mississippi was then somewhat in a state of siege. Tensions were high. The bodies of the civil rights workers had not yet been discovered.

Robert L. Carter, then the NAACP's general counsel and later a federal judge in New York City, Charles Evers, then Mississippi field director of the NAACP and later mayor of Fayette, and I were selected to accompany the committee. Guess who was the first board member to volunteer?

None other than Kivie Kaplan. I tried to dissuade him, pointing out that the president was too valuable to lose on such a journey. But Kivie would have none of it. He insisted on going. Other board members on this memorable trek to segregationland were Dr. H. Claude Hudson of Los Angeles, chairman of the delegation; John F. Davis of East Orange, New Jersey, a youth member; Alfred Baker Lewis of Greenwich, Connecticut; Chester I. Lewis of Wichita, Kansas, attorney; L. Joseph Overton of New York; and Dr. Eugene T. Reed, New York State conference president. We arrived in Jackson, Mississippi, on Sunday, July 5, and were met at the airport by Charles Evers and local NAACP officials. We rented cars for the trip and proceeded into Jackson, where our initial effort to desegregate the city's hotels and motels was successful. The group registered without incident at the King Edward and Heidelberg hotels and at the Sun 'n' Sand Motel in Jackson.

That evening, when the committee addressed a crowded mass meeting at the Pearl Street AME Church, Kivie was one of the featured speakers, explaining the purpose of the trip.

Thereafter, the excitement began, for on the following day the NAACP caravan of board members and press cars journeyed to Canton, where the local police officials were less than hospitable; and then to Philadelphia, the scene of the disappearance of the civil rights workers.

As we entered the courthouse square in the early afternoon and parked our cars in front of the courthouse, we could feel the tension mounting. With Charles Evers leading the way, we entered the courthouse, passing through a gauntlet of hostile local whites in the lower corridor. It seemed as if any one of them would attack Kivie, Alfred Baker Lewis, and Mrs. Lewis, the white members of our group.

As we passed through the lower corridor and mounted the stairs, Kivie passed out "Keep Smiling" cards to the local citizens. You can imagine their chagrin at reading this message; not a smile was noted among them. The committee entered the upstairs courtroom and sought an audience with Sheriff Lawrence Rainey. The sheriff did not see the group, but we did confer with Rayford Jones, county prosecutor, and Cecil Price, deputy sheriff, later indicted for the murder of the civil rights workers.

The conference with Price was tense. Jones refused us permission, as a group, to go to the site of the burned church which Goodman, Schwerner, and Chaney had intended to visit. Robert Carter and Chester Lewis argued that our constitutional rights guaranteed that we could visit the area and that we should be protected. We were told emphatically that our group had no such rights under the federal civil rights laws as understood in that county, and furthermore that local Negroes did not force themselves where they were unwanted.

We should have departed immediately, especially after hearing the word "nigger" and other insulting terms. Carter and Lewis objected strenuously to these epithets and to being called by their first names.

Finally, Kivie spoke loudly to Dr. Hudson, "Claude, you're chairman of this committee and don't you dare leave this room until you get all of the members away because otherwise we'll all go home in boxes." This brought some sense to Carter and Chet Lewis.

When the group left the courtroom it encountered a large, restless crowd of whites inside the building and lining both sides of the street outside. Menacing gestures were made toward the group. It was apparent that the local police were afraid that the crowd might get out of hand, for they did everything they could to speed the NAACP group on its way. As the caravan moved off, it passed a group of Negroes standing apart from the whites; they smiled and waved.

When we got to Moss Point for an evening meeting, there was more hostility. The local sheriff elected to stand in front of the meeting at the Baptist Church with his hand on his gun in an intimidating stance. Rev. R. L. T. Smith, an NAACP official from Jackson, was called upon to give the invocation. In his prayer, he talked scornfully about the sheriff and segregationists in religious terms, but the meaning was clear to the audience who punctuated each sentence with loud "Amens."

After the meeting, we drove to Gulfport to spend the night. The night before had been spent at the Holiday Inn in Meridian. The president of the NAACP's Gulfport branch, Dr. Gilbert Mason, had arranged for the delegation to stay at the beach hotels, which were accepting blacks for the first time. As Kivie and I stood in front of the Edgewater Beach Hotel on the boardwalk, I could see that the local sheriff was very agitated. I asked the branch president about it the next day. He replied, "Mr. Kaplan gave him a 'Keep Smiling' card and attempted to sell the sheriff a life membership."

Kivie later explained the situation to me: "I thought he was a Jewish fellow who owned the motel because he looked like one of my brothers there. So, he opens up his coat with two guns and his badge and you never saw Kivie move so fast in all your life."

The trip was most eventful and full of similar incidents. Kivie's courage was unmistakable.

Each winter the Kaplans went to Florida and remained until spring. While in that state, Kivie always used his time to NAACP advantage by speaking for branches, helping to settle internal organizational problems, and selling life memberships. He would speak for PTAs, churches, interfaith groups, synagogues, as well as NAACP branches.

Kivie was an outspoken foe of black and white racism no matter where encountered.

Kivie Kaplan supported not only the NAACP cause with his time, talents, and money but other civil rights groups as well, including the Congress of Racial Equality and the Southern Christian Leadership Conference.

## 12

# The Man Everybody Knew

*Robert St. John*

*

THE KIVIE Kaplan I knew was a man who in the 1970s was a rara avis — a true liberal in an epoch when acute polarization had driven the extreme left and the extreme right so far apart that they almost bumped into one another, face to face, on the other side of the circle.

The Kivie I knew was a man of positive ideas about a long list of things. He was passionately, articulately, vociferously in favor of a free press, equal rights for all people regardless of skin color, equal rights for all people regardless of sex, good relations with mainland China, decent housing for blacks as well as whites, survival of the State of Israel, abortion for women who desire it, an open door for those who wish to leave the Soviet Union, an intensive program of education designed to lower drug abuse, amnesty for those who went abroad to avoid the draft during the Vietnam War, busing of children in order to achieve school integration, open occupancy on the law books and, in actual practice, more health care for the underprivileged, more social action on the part of individuals, groups, and the government, reform of the way in which convicted criminals are treated in prisons — but most of all he was eager for America, his country, to acquire a moral conscience.

The Kivie I knew was against almost as many things as he was for. He was against anything that smacked of a police state, no-knock police raids, millions of FBI dossiers on law-abiding citizens, ridiculously large military budgets, stupid wars, narcotics abuse, poverty, slums, political corruption, the abuse of any minority by the majority, cutbacks in federal appropriations for social programs, conspicuous consumption, former President Nixon, anti-Semitism, black anti-Semitism, any kind of anti-Semitism, Watergate-type shenanigans, public and private impoliteness, and the behavior of former Vice-President Agnew. The list is long, but these examples are enough to establish the pattern — if there was a definite pattern, which there may not have been for a true liberal like Kivie.

---

ROBERT ST. JOHN *is a noted author.*

Kivie well agreed with Thurman Arnold, a friend of his, who once said:

If I had my way, . . . I would make it a criminal offense for anyone to parade under the banner of liberalism who was not consciously and even religiously devoted to the ideal that, in an industrial democracy, freedom of opportunity is the great value that must be preserved above all things.

It was for the right of black people to have such freedom of opportunity that Kivie gave so much time, thought, and money.

He also agreed with Chester Bowles's statement that "it is the duty of the liberal to protect and to extend the basic democratic freedoms." That, as Kivie saw it, is what the NAACP is all about.

He was very positively in disagreement with the liberal columnist Heywood Broun, who just before he died remarked on his fifty-first birthday: "A liberal is a man who leaves the room when the fight begins." Broun himself was actually not that sort of liberal, and neither was Kivie.

Kivie was amused and somewhat in sympathy with William Gladstone's remark in one of his more famous speeches: "Liberalism is trust of the people tempered by prudence; conservatism is distrust of the people tempered by fear."

Kivie knew Estes Kefauver when he was a senator and applauded Kefauver's statement:

Liberalism means an intelligent effort to keep the political and economic development of our nation abreast of the responsibilities that come from the atomic age. It means an extension of the use of our resources for the common good, the solving of the problem of maintaining democratic principles and free competitive enterprise in a day of Big Business, Big Unions, and Big Government.

The mine workers' leader, John L. Lewis, once said:

It rests with the liberals and the tolerant to preserve our civilization. Everything of importance in this world has been accomplished by the free inquiring spirit and the preservation of that spirit is more important than any social system. That spirit must prevail.

To that doctrine Kivie subscribed.

Walter Lippmann, one of Kivie's favorite political columnists in the forties and fifties, echoed his own feelings with this quotation:

Liberalism has always been associated with a passionate interest in freedom of thought and freedom of speech, in scientific research, in experiment, in the liberty of teaching, in an independent and unbiased press, in the right of men to differ in their opinions and to be different in their conduct.

On the rights of an individual, Kivie always took the position expounded by Wayne Morse when he was senator from Oregon: "The liberal, emphasizing the civil and property rights of the individual, insists that the individual must remain so supreme as to make the state his servant."

The Kivie I knew believed in the sort of brotherhood so well described by Thomas Curtis Clark in his couplet:

Let us no more be true to boasted race or clan,
But to our highest dream, the brotherhood of man.

And Kivie liked the definition of *brotherhood* once expounded by Broun: "Brotherhood is not just a Bible word. Out of comradeship can come and will come the happy life for all. The underdog can and will lick his weight in the wildcats of the world."

The Kivie I knew was volatile, quick to wrath when he felt an injustice had been done, and was intolerant of just one thing: intolerance.

Several years ago he went to Jacksonville for a series of NAACP meetings. During his three days in the city he received half a dozen luncheon and dinner invitations from members of the black community; not one from a white, although his presence in the city had been widely publicized in the papers and on radio and television. "Even my fellow Jews of Jacksonville apparently think the NAACP and I are not quite respectable!" And that was 1972!

In June of 1972 Kivie Kaplan, Dr. S. Norman Feingold (national director of B'nai B'rith Career and Counseling Services), and I went to Jacksonville to receive honorary degrees from Edward Waters College. The president of the college, a majority of the faculty members, and nearly all the students are black. We were met at the airport by two of the black professors and one black administrator and were taken to a motel in the heart of Jacksonville, where reservations had been made for us some weeks earlier by the college.

The reception clerk, white, looked over his glasses at us and our entourage as we tried to register. Finally, rather imperiously, he said: "There are no reservations in the name of Kaplan, Feingold, or St. John."

"Then look under the name of the college!" Kivie commanded, tartly. It was not the first time Kivie had had hotel trouble in the South because he was accompanied by a black or because of his connection with blacks through the NAACP. Finally the reservations were found, but not until both sides of the controversy had made their points.

On the way up in the elevator one of us said to Kivie: "Well, you have to admit anyway that a lot of water has flowed under this bridge in the last ten years or so — blacks, I noticed, are being served in the motel dining room, there were blacks sitting in the lobby, blacks on the motel staff. . . ."

Kivie interrupted: "You'll find that the only black employees in a place like this are doing menial jobs. They're porters, furnace men, cleaners, elevator boys, and maybe — just maybe — waiters. And dishwashers, of course. I doubt if this place has yet had a black guest."

After a pause he spoke what was especially on his mind. "If the hotel had been full, that desk clerk would have been even more arrogant than he was."

Kivie had an easy manner with black people, as well as

with whites. There was no sign of a barrier of any sort — not of color, nor class, nor intellect. He never seemed to be straining to bridge a gap.

"Married?"

"How many children do you have?"

"Boys or girls?"

"Good! I have grandchildren, too."

I can imagine that an archmilitant black might have been turned off by Kivie's attempts at camaraderie. But only an archmilitant would ever accuse him of being patronizing. "We Jews," he once told me, "are in exactly the same situation as the black man, except that our color has made us less conspicuous."

The Kivie I knew, being an extrovert and a very socially conscious man, liked "parties" of all sorts — gatherings of people — weddings, receptions, bar mitzvahs, conventions, conferences, luncheons, dinners, whatever excuse people have for socializing.

It was fascinating to watch the way in which Kivie's various ideological interests became intertwined. Examples are the resolutions NAACP has passed in recent years on the Middle East conflict, the right of Jews to emigrate, and the Austrian chancellor's closing of Schoenau Castle.

Kivie was a born showman. Watching him in action I often thought of the press agent for the Barnum and Bailey Circus who once, when the circus was playing at Madison Square Garden in New York, hired a Bowery character, cut a small hole in one of the pockets of the man's trousers, gave him hundreds of shiny pennies, and started him off on foot for the garden from some East Side intersection like Park and 60th. Of course, by the time the man reached Madison Square Garden he was being followed by hundreds of youngsters who scrambled every time a penny slid through the trouser pocket to the street. (That was in the early days of the century, when a penny had some value. Today the youngsters might even ignore the dribble of small change.)

I thought of the circus stunt every time Kivie handed out one of his famous three-by-four-inch white cards. Some of his quotations read:

Be kind. Remember everyone you meet is fighting a hard battle.

Cooperation is doing with a smile what you have to do anyway.

Temper is what gets most of us into trouble. Pride is what keeps us there.

Nothing is quite so annoying as to have someone go right on talking when you're interrupting.

The man who gets ahead is the one who does more than is necessary — and keeps on doing it.

The most valuable gift you can give another is a good example.

The best way to forget your own problem is to help someone solve his.

Several times, going through airports with Kivie and his wife, I made note of who got the cards. First, the taxi driver who deposited him at the airport. Then the policeman directing traffic if he was within reaching distance. Then the porter who took his bags. Then the man behind the check-in counter. Next, one card each to the men and girls who pawed through the Kaplan carry-on luggage on the theory that maybe this man and his wife were skyjackers. Then the airline employee who made the seat assignments, and the man who opened the door leading to the tarmac, and the girl at the top of the stairs who checked his boarding pass, and finally the stewardesses who served him a meal or a cup of coffee. If there were some way for Kivie to get into the pilot's cabin he would, of course, see that the entire flight crew also got a lesson in smiling. But that not being possible, Kivie used his three-by-fours to break the ice with the passenger beside him or across the aisle.

One of Kivie's Christian friends once said of him: "I am sure that when he gets to heaven he'll hand one of those cards to St. Peter and then to all the archangels."

Once, after attending a convention in Washington, Kivie and Emily on the spur of the moment invited us to have dinner with them in one of the capital's most plush restaurants where reservations are de rigeur. As we entered the establishment, the maitre d'hotel bowed low. "The reservation is in what name?"

Instead of answering, Kivie handed him a "Keep Smiling" card. The imperious headwaiter, who previously looked as if nothing in his life had ever flustered him, stared at the card in some amazement. Then Kivie in his best Bostonian accent said to him: "Read the back side when you have time. [pause] I wrote it myself." Then without putting a period or even a comma into his voice he quickly added "and we would like a very good table for four."

When the wine steward appeared to discuss drinks, Kivie waved aside the formidable wine list and handed the man a "Keep Smiling" card; then he had a lengthy whispered conversation with him — not about anything as routine and commonplace as alcohol: Kivie was giving the wine steward a capsule explanation of his entire philosophy of life. It was all repeated when the waiter arrived to take our food orders. Before Kivie would even condescend to discuss food, he insisted the man read every word on both sides of the card.

The Kivie I knew must have been at some time in his life a member of some sort of "establishment," but he was very antiestablishment in most ways. He often castigated rabbis, priests, and ministers who let the establishment intimidate them and force them into silence when they knew they ought to speak out about the establishment's sins of omission and commission.

He was most impatient with rabbis and other men of

the cloth who tried to disassociate religion and social issues. His belief was that no religion has any meaning or value unless it tries to put its precepts into everyday practice.

Kivie was completely without fear of adopting a minority position on any matter that crossed his field of interest — just as long as he was convinced that he was right.

Long before it was popular to oppose continuance of the war in Vietnam, Kivie was pointing out to anyone who would listen the error of our Southeast Asian policy. He opposed Vietnam whether there was a Republican or a Democrat in the White House.

The best example of Kivie's independence was his attitude toward intermarriage between Jews and non-Jews. Although even the Reform branch of Judaism has taken concerted action to discourage such marriages on the theory that they are one of the chief causes of the declining number of Jewishly religious families in the United States, and although Kivie was an active supporter of Reform Judaism, he retained his own view that mixed marriages are not an unmitigated evil. In long discussions on the controversial subject, Kivie made the point that there are three possibilities open to a Jew and a Christian who wish to get married: (1) they can ask a Christian man of the cloth to marry them, (2) they can ask a rabbi to marry them, or (3) they can get married in a civil ceremony. If they decide to seek out a rabbi, the rabbi should be aware that Judaism has already gained a partial victory, because the couple did not choose one of the other alternatives. If he adamantly refuses to marry them, the two young people, and whatever children they eventually have, may be lost completely to Judaism. By taking such a stand Kivie demonstrated once more his complete independence.

In 1973 it took little courage to be shocked by Watergate and to be critical of those responsible, but, during the rise and fall of Richard M. Nixon, Kivie was fearlessly vocal in his denunciation of the Nixon regime and he would point out: "Remember, I've been a Republican all my voting life!"

It was not the immorality of Watergate that first turned Kivie against the Nixon Administration. It was what he called "the Republican administration's complete lack of understanding of the black man." He often accused Nixon of "shilly-shallying with the law." Kivie was fearless in condemning the Nixonites for lack of racial empathy in their treatment of school desegregation, employment practices, policies in government, housing, "and in every other facet of American life where we have inequalities."

It also took courage to speak out boldly for amnesty and in favor of more lenient abortion laws. On such issues Kivie was always on the side of the young, the liberal, the poor, the antiestablishment people. He had a distinct empathy for youth. In this respect he resembled David Ben-Gurion, Israel's first prime minister. Kivie once told a reporter in Richmond, Virginia: "Young people are beginning to wise up to racial equality. Unfortunately you have to wait for these old bigots to die before the young people come in."

The story got a big play in the *Richmond News-Leader*, with the headline:

NAACP CHIEF'S VIEW:
WAITING FOR OLD BIGOTS TO DIE

Kivie liked to remind black people that American Jews have a long and illustrious record of friendship for them, and that such Jewish leaders as Rabbi Stephen Wise were instrumental in bringing the NAACP into existence; that Rabbi Wise gave it his devoted service for forty years; that not only have two Jews been president of the organization, but many others have served on the NAACP board of trustees and have contributed or helped raise the money to finance its work.

Like many intellectuals, Kivie was also somewhat of a hedonist. He especially enjoyed good food and fine wines. That, in turn, led to a weight problem. By the time each mid-December rolled around Kivie was generally twenty or thirty pounds heavier than his doctor would have liked him to be. But he

had a solution, called Safety Harbor Spa, a place on the Gulf
Coast of Florida, where he spent three months each winter
losing that excess weight and getting back into good physical
trim. This delighted his doctor, but what did not please him
was Kivie's refusal — or inability — to slow down. Every six
months he gave Kivie a more stringent warning, and every six
months the patient faithfully promised the doctor, and Emily,
and anyone else who expressed concern, that he would defi-
nitely shift the Kaplan machine from high gear down into
second. But after a week or two of slowing down he was off
again on his young man's schedule of peregrination, speaking,
conferring, attending, counseling, going, going, going.

The Kivie I knew — like many other busy people — always seemed to find time to answer mail. Often when he was
going off on a three- or four-day trip he would dictate, just
before he left, enough letters to his secretary to keep her busy
throughout his absence. Sometimes they were dispatched with
the notation "dictated but not read by Mr. Kaplan." That line
was unnecessary, for a K.K.-dictated letter was so distinctive
that it could not possibly have been composed by anyone else,
for he dictated as he talked.

Kivie kept up a flowing correspondence with rabbis all
over the country. Many sent him resolutions their congregations adopted on such matters as civil rights and racial situations, as well as copies of their better sermons, which Kivie
often had set into type and sent out broadside. Because he was
well known as a philanthropist, Kivie got almost daily requests
for financial contributions to causes, projects, and even for
the support of individuals whom someone deemed worthy of
help. This was one field in which Kivie believed in discrimination — or at least a high degree of selectivity.

No man likes to be hated. Some of us are disturbed by
even one disrespectful letter among a hundred pieces of fan
mail. Yet Kivie adopted a philosophical attitude toward those
who wrote him castigating letters. And that was a good thing,
because the amateur and professional anti-Semites and those

with a Ku Klux Klan attitude toward black people made him one of their special targets.

Each time Kivie got another scurrilous communication he reminded himself that it is only people who do nothing, who express no positive opinions, and who fight for no causes who are free from attack by the lunatic fringe. Because Kivie fought for so many causes and was intentionally so controversial, over the years he received more hate mail than probably any other public figure since Franklin D. Roosevelt.

(During Grover Cleveland's campaign for the presidency in 1884, his devoted followers created a slogan which they used widely and to good effect: "We love him for the enemies he has made." There are many of us who have said or could have said the same thing about Kivie.)

Sometimes Kivie Kaplan found the attacks so amusing that he made copies and distributed them to his friends. This aroused his supporters to the seriousness of the battle, while at the same time revealing the stupidity and the malice of the enemy.

The rare hate letters which came from people of his own faith did bother Kivie, for he felt that Jews, with their liberal traditions, should be free of such racial prejudice.

Among Kivie's countrywide network of friends were many, both black and white, who dispatched to him any evidence they discovered of bigotry. As a result Kivie had a collection that ought someday to wind up in a museum. One of his favorite examples of the sort of hate he spent his life fighting was a handbill put out by the National Socialist White People's party headed:

UPTIGHT ABOUT SCHOOLS?
OR JUST ABOUT THE NIGGERS?

The leaflet, decorated with Nazi swastikas, read:

Have you "had it" with black animals following you home to beat you up, or pushing your head in the toilet when you go to the john, or "holding" your lunch money for you?

Are you really uptight because white girls have to submit to being "felt up" in the halls by crowds of grinning black monkeys?

If you're uptight about any of these things, you've probably noticed that whenever a white student tries to do anything about it he gets shafted.

On the other hand, the blacks can get away with whatever they want because they stick together and because the gutless school administration is afraid to oppose them.

Conditions in schools have become so rotten that trying to get an education has become a laugh. Who can learn anything caged up with a bunch of cannibals?

They've been telling us for years that niggers are "equal." What a bunch of crap! An administration that believes that is really out of it. As long as they stick together and we don't, we're screwed. But when we learn to stick together, there's nothing we can't accomplish. Let's start learning!

The only way we'll ever have control of our schools again is to organize — and then throw the black scum out into the streets.

Students! Support white self-determination in this school.

Even worse, in Kivie's opinion, was the list of the party's "goals and objectives" printed on the reverse side of the hand-bill.

[It called for an all-white America] in which all children will be beautiful, healthy white babies — never raceless mongrels; an America without swarming black filth in our streets and schools, on our buses, and in our places of work; an America in which our cultural, social, business, and political life is free of alien, Jewish influence; an America in which white people are the sole masters of their own destiny.

Kivie liked to point out how the racists link Jews and blacks, as in this sentence from the same handbill:

We must encourage and promote every form of genuine white cultural endeavor — and at the same time we must break the alien monopoly which exists over our public-opinion-forming media and flush down the drain the poisonous Jewish and Negroid degeneracy which today is passing for "art" and "music" and "literature."

The Kivie I knew enjoyed having an itinerary like a Kissinger. And he liked to boast a little about how mad a schedule he was still keeping, despite the orders of his doctor to slow down or else. . . . This letter was typical:

Emily and I will be going to a wedding on Thursday, then to Indiana for an NAACP meeting, then on the nineteenth to New York for a session of the Religious Action Committee, and on Friday to North Carolina for a conference, and on Saturday we'll be present at a bar mitzvah in Boston.

That, multiplied endlessly, was Kivie's life. Such activity seemed to be the source of his youth and his vitality. And all the while, no matter where or when, he followed the suggestion he made to other people on the front of his three-by-four cards. Intellectually he was constantly concerned with grave problems, yet he faced them with sang-froid and good humor, whether the matter at hand had to do with beleaguered blacks, unwanted Jews, polluted politics, or the need to keep Judaism a living force in the world.

Although honors aplenty came his way, he didn't seem to want or expect acclaim or accolades, nor did he apparently need them to fuel his drive. His motivation came, basically, from his religion. He was a working combination of the aphoristic sayings of Hillel, Confucius, and Ben Franklin.

The Kivie I knew for a twentieth-century retired American businessman had and was a most unusual personality. He tried to practice all the axioms printed on the backs of his three-by-fours. He smiled his way into the lives of blacks and whites alike, all over the world. He was modest and moderate about everything except his devotion to the NAACP, to the Reform movement in Judaism, and to Emily.

In his private life he was extremely conventional. Even in the matter of dress. But he often made behavioral decisions that surprised people. Once when he was invited to a memorial service for Martin Luther King, Jr., he decided not to attend, saying: "I would rather honor the living than the dead."

Kivie not only appreciated the bon mots of others, but he often created epigrams of his own. Among our favorite "K.K.s" (as Ruth and I call them) are:

"The indispensable man has yet to be born."

"Scratch an anti-Semite and you'll generally uncover an antiblack."

Once he told us he considered Evangelist Billy Graham "the chaplain of the status quo."

In the years of his so-called retirement Kivie Kaplan divided his time between three bases of operation: his apartment in Chestnut Hill on the edge of Boston, his summer place on Martha's Vineyard, and Safety Harbor Spa in Florida. He and Emily traveled to and from these places in a car—a large Cadillac with an immense trunk. This trunk was as important in Kivie's affairs as large trunks were for the rum runners in Prohibition days.

Imagine the Kaplans en route from Chestnut Hill to Safety Harbor, a trip of well over a thousand miles which would take them quite a few days, because every hundred miles or so along the way there was a stop to be made — old friends to greet, a cup of tea, a strategy conference, a meal, and usually an overnight stay.

Kivie was not, technically, a politician, but on those trips he planted a great many seeds of his own. He also buoyed up many civil rights friends with his optimism, and as he drove on he always left behind some tangible reminders of his visit. That was the importance of the car trunk.

After the warm greetings were over and Kivie and Emily were settled in their friends' living room, Kivie would excuse himself saying: "Go right on talking; I'll be back in a minute; there's something in the car I want to get."

He discouraged anyone from following him, but those who have peeked have seen that when Kivie unlocked and opened the truck it was full to overflowing (at least at the start of the trip), not with suitcases, clothes, spare tires, or any of the things normal people carry in the trunks of their automobiles, but with what appeared to be the contents of a combination gift shop and bookstore.

Carefully Kivie would select two or three gifts he thought would be most appreciated, close the trunk, and return to the living room with his offerings. By the time he got to the end of his run — Florida or Massachusetts — his trunk would be empty, but he would have left behind a trail of grateful friends who would be thinking of the Kaplans for days, weeks, as they read the books, ate the citrus fruit and candy, and lived with the more permanent gifts.

There was significance to everything Kivie did and significance to all his gifts. Take the Countess Mara neckties. They are either maroon or navy blue and at first glance seem to have an overall design of small fleurs-de-lis, but examined more closely they are not fleurs-de-lis at all but small scales — the scales of justice. One of those ties got me into great trouble during the Watergate hearings. When the Kaplans made their north-south trip in 1972 Kivie presented me with one of his scales-of-justice ties. I thanked him profusely, but after the Kaplan car disappeared down the road I said to Ruth: "I love that man, but he's not very observant or he would have noticed that I have never in all the years I've had a beard worn a four-in-hand tie."

"It would embarrass Kivie to tell him," replied the sometimes very practical Ruth St. John, "so let's just put it away and give it as a present next holiday season to someone who will appreciate it."

And that's exactly what we did. The recipient was a dear friend, Arthur Miller, professor of constitutional law at George Washington University, whose interest in justice was equal to Kivie's.

Some months later, when the Watergate hearings began, Senator Ervin appointed Miller his chief legal consultant on constitutional matters and, several times on television and in newspaper pictures when Arthur was being interviewed or was pictured sitting behind Ervin in the vast hearing chamber, we noticed that he was quite appropriately wearing the scales-of-justice tie. Then one night we got an urgent phone call.

"That necktie you gave me — Senator Ervin noticed it the other day and commissioned me to get him one exactly like it, but Dagmar and I have searched the stores and although we've found plenty of Countess Mara ties not a single one of the shops has ever seen this one with the scales-of-justice design."

"Probably not," I replied, "because I think they were made at the express order of Kivie."

"Kivie? What's Kivie?"

I then had to explain that Kivie is not a *what* but a *who*; a man who . . . and then I had to break down and tell my good friend Miller that his Christmas present really came to him from Kivie Kaplan, that we were only the go-betweens.

"Don't be embarrassed," he replied, "but please, somehow, get another one from your friend, for me to give to Ervin." And we did, after going through the embarrassment of telling Kivie that we had given away one of his gifts.

So it was that one day we all saw Senator Sam Ervin smiling out at the television cameras over a Countess Mara scales-of-justice four-in-hand necktie, a gift from Kivie Kaplan, by way of St. John, via Miller.

The Kivie I knew had the optimism of a very young person. If the three stages of man are youth that lives in the future, middle age that lives in the present, and old age that lives in the past, Kivie qualified as half a middle-ager, half a youth. While he apparently tried to look at life without rose-colored glasses and to see reality for what it actually is, he always wound up any conversation or pronouncement on a hopeful note.

"The trend toward white dropouts from the civil rights front is being reversed," he said not long ago, in a typical burst of optimism. "We're heading toward more racial harmony in spite of rhetoric to the contrary. Progress *is* being made, although, of course, not as fast as I would like to see it."

The Kivie Kaplan I knew and respected lived for years in the vortex of one crisis after another. One day's racial crisis somewhere in the South or in some trouble-torn midwestern city might be succeeded by crisis the next day in Washington, where the military budget was being increased at the same time that appropriations for social programs were being slashed again, while tomorrow's crisis might be in the Middle East, where the Jewish state which Kivie so generously supported in so many ways might be in fresh trouble. But he was accustomed to crises and he confronted each one in turn, contributing time, money, and thought toward a constructive solution.

He was, indeed, a rara avis!

# 13

# A Model for Our Times

## Charles Wesley

*

If one be a hundred years behind one's time, one may remain blissfully unconscious of belatedness. But, if one be a month or three months or a year, as I usually am, ahead of one's time and ahead of events, it is little less than a personal tragedy.

THESE words were written by Rabbi Stephen S. Wise, one of the great rabbinical leaders whose major themes were related to social justice through individual and group participation. He was one of the organizers of the American Jewish Congress and one of the founders of the National Association for the Advancement of Colored People. Few Jewish leaders have spoken and acted with more conviction than he did in his time.

Kivie Kaplan was such a man, in Jewish and black American life. He was neither ahead of his times nor behind them, but going forward with them in a glorious acceptance of his opportunity. In terms of his background, training, and experiences he joined in the group of involvements, representations, relationships, and responses which expressed the needs of his times. He knew that his field of action was not the platform, and yet he was able to make a speech when asked. He believed in the Jewish tradition: "The teaching is not the chief thing, rather the deed." He engaged in deeds primarily, and thus contributed to the legend of his work.

Even when identifying with his own group as an ingroup and with others as outgroups in an advancing and representative democracy, Kivie faced his times with confidence. He carried with him the realization that other peoples were conserving and blending their inner resources and their memories of their past, as in his own case, and discovering that they too were proud of themselves, and he realized that he could work for them and live courageously with them in his times.

DR. CHARLES WESLEY *is executive director emeritus of the Association for Study of Afro-American Life and History.*

The latter period in which Kivie Kaplan lived was different from earlier ones. There was a reduction of anti-Semitism and more acceptance of the policies and programs of his own group. There was a growing, independent Israeli state on its way. There were also African states developing their independence and throwing off colonialism. The United States Supreme Court had rendered its decision in 1954 and 1955 against segregation in the schools and public places, as part of the developing civil rights revolution.

At the same time there were individuals in each group, white and black, who did not want to become involved in the plight of urban centers and rural areas with their decisions in education, housing, crime, and law enforcement. They chose to take refuge within themselves and their families. Where then were those who would follow the models of Wise, Brandeis, Marshall, Frankfurter, Hillman, Lehman, and a host of others on the national and local levels? And yet there were men and women found for these times, and among them was Kivie Kaplan.

Kivie succeeded in finding a place for himself in the field of social justice, not by talking and writing, but by acts of dedication and deeds on behalf of others. He followed in the footsteps of Joel Spingarn and Arthur Spingarn and also joined a host of distinguished Americans in the work of the NAACP. He followed the Jewish tradition in relation to minority peoples.

In 1948 Rabbi Wise wrote to Roy Wilkins, NAACP executive director, concerning a Supreme Court decision in the restrictive covenant cases of Shelly v. Kraemer and Hurdy v. Hodge: "Three cheers for the decision, for which I must tell you the American Jewish Congress, under Shad Polier and Leo Pfeffer, has long been fighting." This statement with reference to the American Jewish Congress was based on historical fact and past relationships. It had worked with the NAACP over the years in many ways, and particularly in the research and publication of *Civil Rights in the United*

*States: A Balance Sheet of Group Relations.* The foreword in 1953 was written jointly and signed by Walter White and David Petegorsky, the former of the NAACP and the latter of the American Jewish Congress. These groups had worked together, joined by many outstanding personalities in this work of social justice.

Kivie Kaplan was one of the forty-eight members of the Board of Directors of the NAACP since 1954. He and Alexander Looby, Nashville attorney, were elected at the same time. This office gave Kivie Kaplan the opportunity to strengthen the financial structure of the organization, and his main area of service was directed toward that goal.

In 1960 the treasurer of the NAACP reported: "Obviously we must not now cut our activities in a crisis period. So we have to raise money by methods which it will be up to the membership to approve." As a result of such views Kivie and his associates in this cause renewed their activity in the 1961 campaign. When it reached the goal of 10,699 members with 1,749 newly enrolled ones, the association was aware that this was a new beginning. The success of this campaign was the result of the work of branches and officers of branches throughout the country and "of the dynamic leadership of National Chairman Kaplan who, not only inspired the committee and the branch workers, but again led in the number of life memberships personally solicited. He continued his efforts even while abroad, enrolling life members while on a trip to Europe and the Orient."

Life memberships have had a long history in the association's annals. On May 14, 1910, in the NAACP's second year, a proposal was introduced for payments of $500 for this purpose. There were discussions of the proposal, and other campaigns were suggested. In 1918 John R. Shilladay, NAACP secretary, was authorized to establish a Legal Defense Fund. In the same year, Mary B. Tolbert, president of the National Association of Negro Women, was appointed to raise $1 million for the NAACP. On January 29, 1927, the NAACP Board of Directors authorized the Executive Committee to draw up a plan for life memberships. A proposal for $1,000 memberships was presented to the board. This was allowed immediately by virtue of payments for that amount by Mary White Ovington and Joel E. Spingarn. Later, $500 life memberships were restored.

When Arthur Spingarn requested that he be permitted to retire in 1966 as president of the NAACP, Kivie Kaplan was elected to succeed him. He had known the value of security in his industrial experiences, and he was aware of the words of Rabbi Samuel Rosenblatt: "There is only one type of security that man can hope for in this world — the ability to face insecurity, to adapt himself to the changing circumstances of time and tide so as not to be overwhelmed by their flood." Kivie had achieved this type of security for himself, and he wanted to achieve it for the association, with its goal of social justice for all its people.

With his cards as a kind of introduction, Kivie began his quest for life memberships. The first two payments were made by John B. Nail, a real estate operator in New York City, whose daughter, Grace, had been married to James Weldon Johnson; and by Dr. Ernest Alexander, a graduate of Fisk University and a New York City physician.

When Kivie Kaplan undertook this specific work for the association he said, "The security of the future depends on the security of today." This concept had been valuable to him in the operation of his company, the Colonial Tanning Company of Boston, and in the management of the Hartnett Tanning Company of Ayer, Massachusetts. He had become a successful businessman through the exercise of prudence, good fellowship, and salesmanship. He sought to use these same approaches in his work for the NAACP.

Kivie Kaplan reported to the life membership luncheon at the 1961 annual meeting in Philadelphia that there were 2,163 fully paid life memberships, bringing in more than $390,000. Kivie Kaplan Life Membership Awards to branches were started in 1958 at the Forty-ninth Annual Convention in Cleveland. Awards were made in 1961 to the branches in Alexandria, Virginia; Boston, Massachusetts; Sacramento, California; Sumter, South Carolina; and Savannah, Georgia. These awards were presented by Kivie himself. In 1972 thirteen branches received such awards, and life memberships were reported in goodly numbers at the annual dinners and luncheons of the association.

Kivie's personal contacts opened many avenues leading to life memberships. He met with rabbis, other leaders in Jewish life, blacks, and his many friends, and discussed his favorite subject with them, asking if they would help pay the cost of freedom. The appeal used by the NAACP was:

> Freedom is not free.
> Its cost is human lives,
> Like Medgar Evers and
> John F. Kennedy
> And the bombed children
> of Birmingham.
>
> Freedom's cost is
> Human sacrifice like that of
> Mrs. Evers and Mrs. Kennedy
> And other grief-felled
> Men and women
> And children.
>
> Freedom's cost is time,
> Endless, unpaid for time.
> Freedom's cost is money,
> Money to erect a tomorrow
> Worthy of those who lived
> And died for it.

Kivie Kaplan regarded himself as involved not only officially but personally in this cause. He continued to make personal commitments to human relations agencies, believing that his faith and work were connected with all of them, but especially to this one. After being elected president at the Detroit NAACP convention in 1972, he said:

I continue to work with the NAACP to practice true Judaism in my everyday life. Remember the NAACP was founded by Jews and Christians, by ministers and rabbis. It is good Christianity to work with the NAACP, just as it is good Judaism.

In this work he had the support of his wife Emily, his three children, and his seven grandchildren. Kivie was a charming host to many whites and blacks in his home, including my wife Louise J. Wesley and my daughter Charlotte Wesley Holloman, a concert artist and a professor of music at the Herbert Lehman College in New York City. The summer residence of the Kaplans on Martha's Vineyard and my daughter's summer residence there have been the scenes of many home-like visits. Charlotte has been presented in benefit concerts for the NAACP.

Kivie broke traditions and taboos, but nevertheless he was making our people his people just as he made our God his God. His dedication to Jewish causes was well known. Brandeis University has a study hall, constructed at a cost of $75,000, in memory of Abraham Lincoln, in the American Civilization Center. It is known as the Emily R. and Kivie Kaplan Lincoln Hall in honor of the donors. Dr. Abram L. Sachar, then president, in announcing this gift, said, "I am delighted with this identification at Brandeis University. Emily and Kivie Kaplan have devoted a lifetime of effort in behalf of others, and the name of Abraham Lincoln is revered by all minority groups. It is fitting that these names should be linked in this fashion."

Kivie's son Edward, a Phi Beta Kappa graduate of Brown University, wrote concerning the march in Montgomery in 1965 in which father, son, and grandson participated together.

A most amazing assortment of people which defied description. I was dazzled, numbed by the vastness, the singing, the determination, the mixture, age and youth, some with suits and ties, others in rags, side by side, under the same sun, the same clouds, marching to the same capital, for the same reasons, priests and nuns, clergy of all sorts, beatniks, farmers, teenage tramps, Ivy League people. This was the exterior.

Edward reported the march through the section where the black schools were located:

[There were] children hanging from the windows to see us, little black children, only black children. Louis was the first to burst into tears. Kivie was the next, as he saw some of the people by the side give cold drinks to the marchers who immediately passed them along after taking a quick gulp.

Edward closed his account as follows:

There we were, three fugitives from the comfortable middle class, well fed abstractionists. We witnessed a magnificently significant example of how our lofty Christian ideals took on the reality of human flesh, black and white, together.

Shortly after this incident Kivie was being escorted by two policemen to the site of the meeting of the NAACP convention in St. Paul. He talked with them and gave them his "Keep Smiling" cards. He asked about their relationship to the movement for equality, and ended by signing them as life members. He was scheduled to make a radio broadcast at the convention, and while waiting his turn at the microphone he approached a news reporter and signed him to a life membership. He spoke to a rabbi with the same result. All this was typical of his tireless and resourceful activity.

Kivie brought forth a new concept of life memberships in the NAACP. His slogan is well known in the association's meetings: "We can exceed our goal if a lot of people do a little." He became known as "the hard-driving cochairman of the Life Membership Committee."

A characteristic incident occurred during one stopover at Montego Bay, Jamaica. It was recounted in a family letter:

There were a colored couple there who seemed to be extremely popular, I didn't know who they were, but I noticed that the gentleman was passing out cards with his picture on it and an autograph. I went over and asked, "May I have one of those cards—I'll give you one of my smile cards?" I found out it was Chuck Berry, the rock and roll artist, who (confidentially) I had never heard of before, and also (very confidentially) he had never heard of me either, so we were even. I found that he came from St. Louis and that he had already enrolled as a life member in the NAACP, but I sold him the idea that he ought to take one out for his wife, to which he agreed very readily.

In all of these relationships, Kivie was following the Torah, which declares that Jews should know the soul of the stranger, for Jews "were strangers in the land of Egypt." His friends were many, all across the country and of all classes and status. He would write or call them and visit them on his travels seeking life members for the NAACP.

His travels for the NAACP led him to tour New York State with attorney Arthur Shores of Birmingham, Alabama; Mississippi with Glouster Current, director of branches, and Maurice White of public relations during the period of the assassination of Medgar Evers and in the mourning period for the family of slain James Cheney; New Orleans, where the *Thunderbolt*, a rabid conservative sheet, referred to Kaplan as "the Jewish Chairman of the NAACP" and as being among the "Jews behind race baiting"; and Florida, where he called publicly for Governor Askew and other officials to plan for representatives on the school boards of the state "at the earliest possible moment, as it was essential for the orderly implementation of school desegregation decisions and recommendations for quality education." In Tipton, Georgia, he called on the NAACP branch to conduct a strong membership drive, stating that he came "to help the economy of Tipton and its surrounding areas."

Kivie Kaplan worked to have whites join the NAACP. He declared:

[The organization should] try hard not to practice what we're fighting against—racism. The NAACP must welcome and invite white members more than ever. White bigots are doing all within their power to keep Jews and blacks at each other's throats. Problem anti-Semites are violently antiblack. In fact it should be well known that no minority is safe when another minority is unsafe.

In his book *Basic Reform Judaism* (1970) Rabbi William B. Silverman's dedication reads:

Kivie and Emily Kaplan whose devotion to social justice exemplifies the prophetic ideals of Reform Judaism in action.

The author ends his book with questions and answers. He asks, "When will the night end? How will we know when it is light?" And he replies:

We will know when it is light when we are able to see the face of our brother, when we can look upon the face of a human being and not see the face of a Jew or a Christian, Muslim or pagan, not the face of a black man, or a white man, or yellow man, but when we, through our faith, can look upon a human being and see the face of a brother as a child of God, then we will know that there is the dawning of a new and resplendent light and we will prepare to advance into the world to come a moral society of universal justice, brotherhood, and peace.

Few whites have translated their religion into the life of their times with the effectiveness of Kivie Kaplan, and few blacks have done it. He was able, with his religious background, to live and work with peoples of all faiths, Jews and non-Jews, Christians and non-Christians, black and white, rich and poor, privileged and underprivileged, the happy and the troubled. He became to all of them the legend of a good man. He went forward in our time with the confident expectation that the prophetic dream just noted will become a reality.

# 14

# A Man Who Is "For Real"

## *DeLores Tucker*

\*

I HAVE a little book called *Treasury of Jewish Thoughts*, to which I often turn. As I read and ponder the gems of wisdom therein, I think of Kivie Kaplan, not because he gave me the book, but because its overall spirit seems to sum up the essence of this remarkable man. I did not know Kivie when he was a youth or young man, but it is clear that he must have taken these thoughts to heart long ago and vowed to live by them.

Adlai Stevenson said of Eleanor Roosevelt that she would rather light one small candle than complain of the darkness. Kivie was in the great Eleanor Roosevelt tradition — the proud tradition of what we call "old-fashioned liberals" — people unusually endowed by God with intelligence, position, and material comfort who believe it is their responsibility to use those gifts by working ceaselessly for others.

The midrash says "many candles can be kindled from one candle without diminishing it." While Kivie's own candle burned brightly of itself, he magnified it a hundredfold by spreading its flame to kindle more and more candles near and far. I think of the thousands of plain, ordinary people he has sustained and encouraged and comforted all over this nation — just how many, none of us will ever know. "Deeds of kindness," the Talmud says, are "equal in weight to all the Commandments."

Kivie's life spanned more than seven decades, and they must all have been good years — difficult sometimes, heartbreaking sometimes, but always imbued with that indomitable joyous spirit synonymous with Kivie Kaplan. "The Holy Spirit rests upon him who has a joyous heart," the Talmud tells us. To look at Kivie was to see a man who had achieved that tranquility, a man at peace with himself and his God, a man determined to share that peace and happiness with all.

---

DR. DELORES TUCKER *is secretary of state of the Commonwealth of Pennsylvania.*

I never saw Kivie without a smile on his face, never saw him angry, never saw him when he wasn't actively trying to pass along his blessings.

The Talmud teaches that "charity knows neither race nor creed." I think this was something Kivie never had to be taught. In whatever country or era he lived, he would have recognized this bond with the downtrodden. And he would have done something concrete about it, as he did for over forty years.

Kivie devoted himself to ending the inhumanity of some of God's children to others. "Love therefore the stranger, for you were strangers in the land of Egypt."

None of God's children were strangers to Kivie, but I think he felt a special affinity for blacks. "We Jews and you blacks are in the same situation," he once told me, "except that our color makes us less conspicuous." Well, Kivie certainly made himself conspicuous in his efforts to help us.

To say that the black movement was enriched by Kivie Kaplan would be a gross understatement. He, and other great white liberals like him, truly made it possible for the NAACP to be born, to grow and prosper, and to yield an influence on the legal and social structure of this land to an extent un-equalled by any other civil rights organization anywhere in the world. Kivie, as the latest ardent white spokesman at the helm of the NAACP, not only made his own lasting contribu-tion, but assured the continuation of the organization's growth by concentrating on the young people who must carry the responsibility for its future expansion. Youth membership in the NAACP rose fifteen percent in the last three years of his presidency, and that trend promises to accelerate.

Turning back to my *Treasury of Jewish Thoughts*, I find a quotation from Pirke Avot: "Who is wise? He who learns from all men." And Kivie learned! He not only liked people but he found them fascinating. So he listened — and learned — and understood. And he usually ended up knowing more about them than they did about him.

Most people who are at all familiar with the black movement are aware of what Kivie accomplished in the field of fund
raising at critical moments in our civil rights history. He not
only gave lavishly himself but persuaded others to come
forward and "put their money where their mouth is." Here is
another case where Kivie was a living example from that little
book of holy precepts: "If one can induce others to give, his
reward is greater than the reward of the one who gives." I
doubt that Kivie was ever even remotely tempted to do good
for the sake of reward.

During the years that Kivie and I were associated in
NAACP work we continually corresponded, and I have kept
and treasured his letters. I think they give the truest picture
of his great qualities of heart and mind and soul. I include a
few of the most recent.

The first is a typical example of his interest in others,
his generosity of feeling, love of family, backbreaking work
schedule, and unswerving commitment to civil rights:

June 25, 1972

Dear DeLores:

I think you can imagine my happiness and pride in seeing
the wonderful article in the July *Ebony* about you, and I certainly
want to again congratulate you on the wonderful work that you
have been doing for so many years. It really is wonderful, DeLores,
that we have people with the guts and courage and ability like
you who are willing to stand up and be counted and make a record
that all of us can be so proud of.

I can remember many years ago when you and I were so
vitally interested in our national life membership program. I
don't remember the 1965 March to Montgomery whether or not I
saw you, but I was happy and proud that I was there with my
son and my grandson. We had three generations, and it was one
of the great events of our lives, and I am sure that none of the
three of us will ever, ever forget it.

I am also pleased that last April, I just rounded out forty

years with the NAACP and that we now have over 50,000 life members, having started with only 221.

On the other side, we have so much work to do, DeLores, that the days just don't seem long enough and those of us who believe must continue to work very, very hard.

It isn't easy for me to keep going as fast as I am going but I just can't sit down and rest, with so much to do.

After we left after three days in Philadelphia, we had five days in Mississippi, which included an honorary degree that I received at Saints Junior College and gave the Commencement Address; since then, I've had six days of meetings in New York and finished up with participation in the naming of the school for Dr. Ralph J. Bunche, May his Soul rest in Peace. His wife and Emily and I have been friends for many, many years and in that capacity, as well as president of the NAACP, I was on the program.

On June 30th I leave for Detroit where, as a result of having invited many rabbis to the ministers breakfast, I've been invited to speak at one synagogue on Friday evening services on June 30th; another on Saturday morning services July 1 and I usually speak at a church the day before the convention and I'll be getting back to Martha's Vineyard late on July 8.

I am sure that with all of us working together we can do a lot more, but the job is to get others on to the team. I know you are doing everything within your power to do this, and God bless you and your husband with good health, peace, and contentment.

Emily joins in sending these congratulations and best wishes,

Yours for equality,

Kivie

My reply alludes to the growing clamor by some blacks that only a black person should be president of the NAACP. I strongly opposed this concept, standing firmly on the position that any person who had contributed as much to the black cause as Kivie Kaplan had and would continue to have my support until a black came along who could match him.

July 19, 1972

My dear friend:

How pleasant it was to see you again at the national meeting in Detroit and to see you steadfastly warming everyone with your glowing smile and smile cards, while encouraging everyone to buy or sell life memberships.

No matter what some small minds and voices espouse, there has been no one, black or white, who has contributed any more to the life of the NAACP than our own beloved president, Mr. Kivie Kaplan. When a man or woman, black or white, can produce a record of service equal to yours, then, and only then, does he or she have the right to challenge your presidency of our great organization. When will humanity ever learn that God is the Father of us all and that He created humankind in all varieties; not only humankind, but there is no living organism that He did not create in variety. Therefore, God must have loved variety and found beauty in it, and so should all humankind.

Following the NAACP convention, I attended the National Democratic Convention which was held in Miami Beach, where I was asked by Senator Muskie to second his nomination. Although I am disappointed that my candidate, Mr. Muskie, did not win the nomination, I do think that Senator McGovern is a good, compassionate man concerned about people and human issues rather than the issues of war and space. Quite evident at the convention was his remarkable ability to generate a zealousness on the part of youths, women, and minorities to really become involved in the political process of our nation. This is good and I have faith that he can overcome and retire Mr. Nixon to San Clemente in January 1973.

To many, the NAACP convention certainly charted the direction that the NAACP and all its allies must follow and heralded a clear trumpet call to march on till victory is won.

I am convinced, as I tell my audiences, that the NAACP is the hope for returning this government to a moralistic and humanistic concern for the people of this nation and the world. Despite all criticisms against the NAACP, I say to all groups that I speak to that the NAACP is ALL WE HAVE. SCLC, CORE, and SNCC are gone, and so we must all—people of good will, black and white—join in with all the resources at our command to assist the NAACP in making this nation truly the land of equality and justice for all.

Bill and I send you and Emily our warmest best wishes for a joyous and relaxing summertime. Truly, you are both the most activist couple in the Army for Freedom.

Yours in peace, freedom, and love,

C. DeLores Tucker

His response was quick and heartwarming:

July 25, 1972

Dear DeLores:

Your letter of July 19th was a great boost for me although you know I am an eternal optimist and I never get discouraged. Working with the NAACP for over forty years, you cannot ever, ever get discouraged: but your letter really gave Emily and me a great boost and I am sending it to Mr. Muse in New York to show him, and, if you have no objection, I would certainly like to show it to others.

A later letter shows again his great gift of friendship and the grueling pace he set for himself as long as there was work to be done for the cause:

March 8, 1973

Dear DeLores:

I hope this letter finds you and your husband well and that everything is going along nicely.

I was certainly pleased and proud to see in the March 1st *Jet* the Public Service Award of the United Bankers of America that you received, and I am positive that you deserve this much, much more for your years and years of dedicated service to the fight for human dignity that you and I are so vitally interested in, and keep up the wonderful work! We need more DeLores Tuckers in this fight which is so important for all of us.

I've been keeping extremely busy, probably a little bit too much so, speaking for NAACP branches within a radius of 120 miles so I could come back the same night, human relations groups, church and temple groups, migrant workers, PTA meetings, etc. We leave here on March 10th for our drive homeward and, that same night, I'll be speaking for the Jacksonville branch, then continuing on to Atlanta; from there we fly to San Antonio, Texas, from March 15th to the 18th, and to Dallas from the 18th to the 21st; then to Greenville, South Carolina, for our regional convention from the 21st to the 25th, and, from there, we'll continue on our drive homeward which will bring us back to Chestnut Hill about the first of April.

I thought you would like to see the article from the *St. Petersburg Times* enclosed herewith.

With best to all in which Emily joins,

Sincerely yours,

Kivie

After I spoke to the New England Regional Conference at the invitation of President Kenneth Guscott, I received the following communication from Kivie — that vital and indefatigable "humanician." It shows the same spirit of caring and sharing, his never-ending concern for the civil rights movement and his obliviousness to the physical toll such unceasing activity must have cost him.

October 7, 1973

Dear DeLores:

It was certainly wonderful to see you and your husband both looking so well, and, as usual, you were certainly wonderful in your presentation to our people.

I think you felt as badly as I did with the small number of life members who stood up who said they would take out life memberships, which shows we have a lot of work to do.

You will excuse me for rushing away without saying goodbye because the doctor wants me to slow down and live, as I have been overdoing for the prior four months to my going to Martha's Vineyard for the summer, and I was very ill there the entire summer and did nothing but rest, take pills, and see the doctor. Although I had made prior commitments before I became ill, I felt I wanted to keep them so, when we returned from Martha's Vineyard August 31st, I was in New York for two and a half days for the Board and Committee meetings, then to Washington for the Watergate situation for a day and a half, to which I took my grandson Barry Green, then I had five days in New York and Beaver Valley, Penn., where I spoke to a Friday evening joint service of two congregations, a Conservative and a Reform, and then the Freedom Fund dinner of the Beaver Valley NAACP. This last weekend, Emily and I went to Peabody, Mass., for the New England Regional Conference, and from then on I am turning everything else down and I am going to try and take it easy, but, with mail, telephone calls, and visitors, it isn't quite that easy.

I am wondering if you have any suggestions as to how we can approach the Armed Services personnel, officers, and enlisted men for regular and life memberships because I've had experiences at different branches where I have been able to sign a lot of them up, but you know you can only visit so far and do so much; and I am wondering whether you might come up with a suggestion as to how we can get them by mail and really get a lot of them.

Emily joins in sending love to you and your husband, and with our greatest admiration for the job well done, and best wishes for good health, peace, and contentment,

Yours for equality,

Kivie

Perhaps the most amazing thing of all about this amazing man is that he was "for real." In a nation of people concerned with images, postures, stances, and the creation of desired effects, Kivie Kaplan was exactly what he seemed to be.

I was proud to call him friend.

# 15

---

# What I Preach,
# He Practiced

## *Samuel Silver*

\*

W HAT I preach, he practiced.
Many a clergyman has had occasion to use that phraseology in connection with some altruist in his congregation. Of no one is it truer than of Kivie Kaplan. He was the incarnation of goodness.

What he had in the way of worldly goods was the result of his energy, enthusiasm, and business skill. With his worldly goods he took seriously the Judeo-Christian legacy which says that a man must share what he has with those in need. He was the ideal philanthropist in the literal sense of that term, which means love of one's fellow human being.

It was my good fortune to be a neighbor of the late Jackie Robinson. His great claim to fame was that, after black athletes had been barred for decades from major league baseball, he was the first to break the barrier, thus opening the way for others. But Jackie and his beloved wife Rachel also devoted their energies to the performance of other good deeds. One of the most significant was their work of signing up life members for the National Association for the Advancement of Colored People.

In this effort, which took Jackie across the country many times, into the offices of many men of influence and affluence, he was Kivie's partner. Jackie often told me that the spectacular leap in the number of life members of the NAACP from hundreds to thousands was due to the exertions of Kivie Kaplan. The latter, of course, modestly gave the credit to the famed athlete.

Some individuals use high posts for the accumulation of power. But Kivie used the presidency of the NAACP only to widen the orbit of his services. In his typical fashion, he traveled and traveled, spoke and pleaded, in cities throughout the United States. He went into the most bigoted spots in the country and reminded the followers of Moses and the fol-

SAMUEL SILVER *is rabbi of Temple Sinai in Stamford, Connecticut.*

lowers of Jesus that the translation of their theologies must
be in terms of everyday deeds which reflect their understanding of the essential familial bond that ties together all the
children of God.

It was not only the matter of his mission but the manner
in which he executed it that electrified thousands of his friends.

He responded to hostility with graciousness.

His cherubic countenance maintained its brightness
whether he was with his beloved battlers for dignity in a black
agricultural colony in Mississippi or with a pride of hatelers
in Bigotsville.

He was patient with the convinced and the unconvinced.

He gave endless interviews to newspaper reporters.

No national president of a major organization was more
accessible to the press than Kivie Kaplan.

And no matter how he was treated, he was imperturbable.

When, for example, the reporter of a paper whose editorial policy was notoriously xenophobic took hours to ask him a
series of questions, Kivie painstakingly "fielded" all of them.
When the interview was over, Kivie said quietly to the reporter, "You realize, of course, that not a word of this interview will appear in your paper." The reporter denied it, but
the prediction proved correct. And yet, when Kivie later told
this anecdote, his face was bright with laughter.

When you met him, you would naturally bring him up to
date about yourself. He listened carefully, and then, with incredible mnemonic prowess, he asked about all of your relatives and friends, forgetting nary a name.

A "soft touch," Kivie found it difficult to say no. Those
who came to him for assistance on behalf of noble purposes
rarely got a refusal.

He must also have been the greatest granter of favors in
the nation. He got countless pleas for references, recommendations, aid of all kinds, and he kept busy granting these
requests when he could.

To see Kivie at his happiest was to see him with his

family. He may have spent the day lecturing or dictating letters to a secretary, but when leisure time came, either in Martha's Vineyard in the summer or Safety Harbor Spa, Florida, in the winter, he was all aglow as he relaxed. If you were just a friend, you soon felt as though you were a member of the family circle.

And before telling you about the new victory won for the cause of desegregation, he'd tell you about the latest article written by his scholarly son, Edward, or about the latest exploits of his grandchildren.

Kivie Kaplan's lifelong struggle on behalf of black people takes its place with such Jewish striving for equality as the wholesale largess of Julius Rosenwald (who made gifts to black YMCAs), the spirited advocacy of a Maurice Eisendrath, and the contributions of many other Jews who felt that the cause of black persons was something to which every Jew was obligated to lend a hand.

But Kivie Kaplan's aid to the blacks transcends what the latter received from Rosenwalds and Eisendraths, because he had to withstand the rigors of the backlash. By backlash is meant the resentment of many blacks of white (and Jewish) involvement in the battle for color equality. Separatists among the blacks scorned and spurned white collaboration. This reverse bigotry reached into the NAACP. Its waves sometime even swirled into the office of the presidency.

In the light of this phenomenon, many Jews gave up their enthusiasm for the struggle to bring equality to blacks. They said: "If you don't want us, we'll leave you." And leave the struggle many did.

True, Eisendrath didn't falter. But Kivie was in the eye of the hurricane. He had every reason to say, "OK, you don't like the color of my skin. Fine. Take over yourself." To his everlasting credit, he remained stalwart in support of the black cause even while many others fell away.

Kivie Kaplan did not enroll in the fight for equality because he wanted gratitude but because he felt the prophetic mandate to do so. He remained in the cause because it was right. As the discussion raged, he received blows both from blacks who were fed up even with the friendly "Big White Father" and from Jews who said, "Look here, Kivie, you've done enough for the blacks. Now give of yourself and your means for your own."

Kivie Kaplan saw all too keenly that the centuries-old gulf between what blacks should have gotten and what they have gotten had not been materially reduced. He knew full well that the victories won for the cause of racial decency were not yet substantial enough to make up for the deficiencies of that long epoch during which blacks were in the substrata of American life.

There is too much that still has to be done. In spite of protests from both sides, Kivie Kaplan clung to those measures which will make the dreams of his erstwhile companion, Martin Luther King, Jr., come true.

In Hebrew, the word *kaplan* is a homonym for "double." This man Kaplan was endowed with a double portion of saintliness, and this world, through him, has been doubly blessed.

# 16

## The Glory of Kivie Kaplan

*Edward W. Brooke*

*

LAWYERS have been the *sung* heroes of the National Association for the Advancement of Colored People. Their legal scholarship, ingenuity, persistence, and magnificent advocacy are all a cherished ballad in the still unfinished struggle to make the United States Constitution's mandate — freedom, equality, rule of law — a reality for black Americans.

Kivie Kaplan was not a lawyer; he was not in the front lines of those epic, necessary legal battles. But Kivie was a giant and a general in the NAACP's ranks all the same. Behind the front lines, quietly. He earned every medal the association could bestow.

I met Kivie in the early 1950s. I had finished law school at Boston University, married, begun the practice of law in Roxbury, and was about to take my first, hesitant steps into the swift stream of Massachusetts politics.

The Boston chapter of the NAACP was particularly active in the still comparatively small (but long since established) black community. Kivie Kaplan was already a pillar in that organization. He had achieved the status of successful businessman. He could have, as many do, settled for that and his happy family life. He could have slowed down, relaxed more, worked less, and even found some spare time for a good cause.

Kivie had other ideas. He didn't talk the grandiloquent language of "mission." He made no dramatic speech or announcement. But he quietly decided and set upon a new career — not an avocation, a *career* — to help bring about dignity and equality for black Americans.

Kivie enlisted and invested more and more of himself until he became a full-time worker in what, much later, became known as the civil rights movement.

His apprenticeship included almost every local and state leadership position. He listened. He learned. He taught. A

---

EDWARD BROOKE *is US senator from Massachusetts.*

younger generation watched and listened to this strong, smiling, dedicated man, and then still another generation.

Kivie's talents had long since burst the bounds of Boston
and the state of Massachusetts. He had the integrity and the
quality which a growing, active, yeasty national organization
needs. He knew that numbers and dollars equal effectiveness.
And he charted for himself and the NAACP the course to
acquire both.

Life memberships in the organization seemed to Kivie
an especially effective way to strengthen NAACP's sinews for
battle. With patience and unflamboyant, unflappable zeal,
Kivie set himself the task of adding to (no, multiplying!)
that category of membership.

He wrote. He traveled. He talked. He called. Day after
day, month after month, year after year. And the life membership rolls multiplied — giving the organization the financial
strength it needed for the great legal confrontations of the
sixties.

In 1960 I made a decision to run for statewide office in
Massachusetts. I had no organization, no money, no statewide
political track record. What I had — in marvelous abundance
— were a few friends like Kivie Kaplan whose counsel, steadfast loyalty, and insight into the political process enabled me
to poll more than a million votes, albeit in a losing cause.

When I ran for the Republican nomination for attorney
general of Massachusetts in 1962, I was able successfully to
build on the foundation which Kivie had — in typical, quiet,
selfless fashion — helped me lay in 1960.

The 1962 campaign was my toughest; I should say *our*
toughest.

The nucleus of my campaign organization was old Rox-
bury/NAACP/AMVET and newer Republican friends who
shared with me the ups and downs of what amounted to three
separate and distinct electoral endeavors. We first had a state
convention to win. That battle was and is remembered as a
Massachusetts classic: the first-ballot results were one vote

short (out of almost 2,000) of giving Elliot Richardson the convention's endorsement. I was nine votes behind, while (now) Judge Arlyne Hassett held a small but decisive block of nine votes.

We were resilient and resourceful, and on the second ballot we rallied. We won a stunning, substantial victory. As I remember it, Kivie and Emily Kaplan were in the gallery sitting near my mother and father, cheering, praying, and probably even crying a little when — after the first ballot — things looked grim for us.

Since that hot, steamy afternoon in the Worcester Auditorium, fifteen years ago, hundreds of people have had occasion to greet me, press my hand, and assure me that "I was that one vote in Worcester." The wonderful thing was and is that every single person has been right: each *was* the decisive Brooke first-ballot vote.

Kivie was never active in partisan politics and wasn't a delegate that day. But I have no doubt that he, too — somewhere along the line — corralled, cajoled, or converted a vote — *the* vote — several votes.

In the primary and general election that followed, we had hectic but less hair-raising campaigns — and more emphatic, decisive, immediate affirmative results.

As attorney general of Massachusetts for four years, and since as a United States senator, I have been on the firing line of decision. Constantly. Kivie's advice, whether expressed in person or by mail (he was an inveterate, literate letter writer), was always pithy and prescient. He cut through — in simple common sense, but eloquent words — to the heart of any public policy matter.

Like so many other old, affectionate friends the world over, we didn't see one another often enough. But since we shared a love for Martha's Vineyard — that nonpareil island of beauty and brotherhood just off the southeastern coast of Massachusetts — our paths were most likely to cross in summer. I would be up for a short or hopefully long weekend for a change of pace from the rollcalls, hearings, and ongoing schedule of almost year-round congressional sessions. Kivie was resting, too — from an extended trip to the South or West, from this conference or that regional meeting.

We picked up our conversation and friendship just where we last left off: the shared memories, the shared involvement in a cause we deeply believed in, the shared love of people and American institutions.

Kivie Kaplan was my friend. A wise man and a good man who without the sound of trumpets, *with*, instead, innate modesty, caring, and commitment, helped to make brotherhood, civility, and the mandate of the Constitution more of a reality in our country. In those years of crisis, confrontation, and conflict he never faltered, never doubted, never was faint of heart or slow to act.

Kivie — for too long — was an *unsung* hero. He liked and wanted it that way.

But the record is written. *It* sounds the trumpets. It records the giving and the glory of Kivie Kaplan.

# 17

# Vignettes

*

# Kivie's Point of View

*Harry Golden*

SOME YEARS ago Kivie Kaplan of Boston, Massachusetts, gave up his business, the Colonial Tanning Company, the world's largest producer of patent leather. He turned
the business lock, stock, and barrel over to his employees,
twenty percent of whom were black. Kivie did this because he
said he must "march with the Negroes."

Almost every newspaper photograph of Dr. Martin
Luther King, Jr., leading a protest march in Selma, Alabama,
or Jackson, Mississippi, or other crisis cities of the nation
always showed Kivie Kaplan marching beside Dr. King. Kivie
interpreted Judaism to be a struggle for social justice, and that
is what motivated the man — social justice.

He told the Negro audiences, "Six million human beings
were incinerated virtually without protest from the rest of
the world. I know what suffering is — mine and yours."

He worked "twelve to fifteen hours a day for the NAACP
and the Union of American Hebrew Congregations Social
Action Commission."

I was sitting with him on the platform in Los Angeles
when one of George Lincoln Rockwell's violent anti-Semitic
people attempted to attack him physically. In a speech, Kivie,
addressing himself to alleged Negro anti-Semitism, said:
"Whether some Negroes are or are not anti-Semitic is peri-
pheral to the question of whether the Negroes should walk in
dignity and that their children should be uninhibited in their
search to find their place in this society." And so this good
man, Kivie Kaplan, in making sometimes five speeches a
week, to white and Negro audiences, was following the lesson

HARRY GOLDEN *is the author of
many popular books.*

he learned from his parents and grandparents about translating Judaism into action for social justice.

"I was taught by my parents and my religion that, if God was good to me and provided me with worldly goods, it was intended that I be only an agent for them and distribute them to my fellow man."

He also noted that "the John Birch Society spent $3 million last year fighting equality of opportunity for all men. . . . The least those of us who believe in equality could do is try to match that kind of money."

# As Seen by a WASP

## Lois Mark Stalvey

K IVIE KAPLAN'S enormous achievements in *minority* group betterment are internationally known; his impact on one WASP family, ours, seems of insignificant interest by comparison. It is worth telling, I believe, because many people can achieve recognition in large, public gestures. Only a small number of thoroughly good people are consistent in even the smallest, day-to-day matters.

Kivie and our family met on paper. He had read a copy of my first book, *The Education of a W.A.S.P.*, and wrote to say he liked it. I shared his letter with my husband, Ben, and we shared it with our three nearly-teenaged children.

Kivie came across life-sized and alive in his letters, and soon our children felt they, too, knew him. Letters from 280 Boylston Street were grabbed by Spike, Noah, and Sarah. When Kivie sent up a copy of the infamous *Thunderbolt* newspaper with its virulent hatred of black people and Jews, we considered this a good opportunity to show our children — especially our oldest, Spike, then fourteen — an example of a hate publication. Being reared in an integrated neighborhood with a large number of Jewish families, our WASP children, we felt, might not realize that not all people accept and understand one another. When Spike read the article attacking Kivie, he looked puzzled. I reread it and, with amusement and amazement, realized that Spike could not understand that just being called a Jew was, to anti-Semites, insult enough. Everything the *Thunderbolt* was attacking Kivie for doing — aiding, "race-mixing," *being* a Jew —was to Spike something laudable. The *Thunderbolt* didn't make sense to our son; Kivie did.

LOIS MARK STALVEY *is author of numerous books.*

But the influence of Kivie on our children transcended the matters of "race" and religion. Inevitably, curious teen-agers had to ask deeper questions about life. And they came: "Why is Mr. Kaplan so nice?" "Why is he so helpful to everybody?" It may have been our middle child, Noah, who asked me, but the other two listened raptly.

As I tried to explain Kivie to my children, I knew I was describing, through one person, all the values and ideals we hoped they would incorporate into their own lives. These three modern kids would not hold still for vague phrases and platitudes, but learning about a man they had grown to know — this they understood.

I explained that there are a few special people who know that helping others is the real way to happiness, and Mr. Kap-lan was one. That, one day, he decided that just making more money was not important and he then began to *give* his time to people who needed it. I said he gave money, too, but that was not as important as giving his time and his concern and his heart.

And as I talked to my children about the specific things Mr. Kaplan did (all of which are well documented in this book), I began to realize that, through Kivie, my husband and I had adopted new ways of thinking and living. Those "Keep Smiling" cards Kivie distributed contained phrases that had made us change, and by changing had made us better models for our children. We did remember that "everyone you meet is fighting a hard battle," and I had often smiled, shrugged, and reminded myself that "cooperation is doing with a smile what you have to do anyway."

For our family, Kivie had lived — and taught these two parents to live — his most important printed suggestion of all: "The most valuable gift you can give another is a good ex-ample." This gift from Kivie to us — and, we hope, to our children — will keep this one WASP family in his eternal debt.

# His Work for Unity

## Robert T. Coleman

I FIRST met Kivie about ten years ago, when he was a member of the board of Hatzaad Harishon, a New York–based organization of multiracial Jews whose goal was to facilitate the integration of black Jews into the social and religious life of the larger Jewish community. I remember stressing to Kivie the fact that many of the blacks whom he wanted to "integrate" were not Jewish according to Jewish religious law. To which he quipped, "I'm not sure that all of the white Jews would qualify by the standards you've set forth." Needless to say, his reply had the effect of making me, a black Jew, feel as though I were a staunch conservative.

In 1970, when I joined the staff of the Synagogue Council of America as director of its Department of Social Justice, the first congratulatory note I received bore the signature of Kivie Kaplan who took the opportunity to express his concern that the American Jewish community was retreating from the struggle for social justice for blacks.

Kivie found this "retreat" on the part of Jews, and the anti-Semitism expressed by some black militants, very painful since he had dedicated his life to trying to bring the two groups together in an effort to stamp out racial and religious prejudice.

There was hardly a time when I met with Kivie and his wife and comrade-in-arms, Emily, that he did not discuss this problem and express the belief that the NAACP could find meaningful solutions if blacks and Jews would join hands in seeking them.

---

ROBERT COLEMAN *was director of the Department of Social Justice of the Synagogue Council of America.*

Kivie's conviction that blacks and Jews should be natural allies did not always ingratiate him with either group, to say nothing of the poisonous hate mail he received from white citizens' councils and the Ku Klux Klan over the years.

At a recent meeting with Kivie and Emily, I discussed the great work that the Lubavitcher Rebbe, a renowned chasidic Jewish leader, was doing to bring Jewish youth back to Judaism. When I told him of the warm acceptance every Jew, regardless of skin color, received at the Crown Heights headquarters of the Lubavitcher Chasidim, Kivie replied: "Good, now get the rebbe to take out a life membership in the NAACP." When I tried to explain to Kivie that the rebbe was called upon to give to a tremendous number of charities, he said, "He can pay it off."

In May 1973 the Synagogue Council of America held a consultation with black Jewish leaders from all over the United States in an attempt to have black and white Jewish communities explore some of the problems that separate the two groups. Among the speakers were several blacks who advocated separatism and made all kinds of accusations against white Jews. When the last speaker had concluded his remarks, Kivie ascended the dais and made an impassioned plea for the two groups to work more closely. His off-the-cuff pleas touched the hearts of all, and today many of us are working toward the goals he so passionately advocated.

# Kivie and Integrated Housing

*Morris Milgrim*

I looked on Kivie as a modern-day John Brown, using non-violent techniques of gentle persuasion to achieve the same vital results John Brown attempted years ago. His goal was not only to free the slaves but also to improve the conditions of blacks and poor people generally.

You may be interested in learning how I met Kivie and how he had a *major* effect in developing integrated housing in America.

It is my custom to pick up every hitchhiker I pass as a matter of principle, as part of my effort to live the golden rule.

About 1956 I picked up two young black lads who asked for work. I gave them work on one of my first integrated housing developments, as one of them lived across the street. I found out that his sister was secretary of the NAACP Life Membership Committee and occasionally when I drove to New York I gave her a lift there. This young lady became interested in my work. She told Kivie about me and arranged for us to have dinner in New York.

Kivie listened as I told him (around the fall of 1957) of my pioneer efforts to develop integrated housing both at Concord Park and Greenbelt Knoll and later at two developments at Princeton, New Jersey. I suggested that he might like to invest a million dollars in my new national company to develop integrated housing. He responded that he knew nothing about housing but that his son-in-law, Mort Grossman, did, and that I should visit with Mort.

I had lunch with Mort Grossman in Boston and spent several hours with him. At about 8 P.M. we had dinner with

MORRIS MILGRIM *is president of* Partners in Housing, *Philadelphia.*

Kivie, who had returned exhausted from a major conflict of wills in his company which he had resolved successfully. Kivie asked Mort if he should invest $25,000 in my company, Modern Communities Developers. Upon Mort's approval, Kivie promptly wrote a $25,000 check. I waved that around in several places and got three more like it. It was this first $100,000 on which Modern Communities Developers was founded in 1958.

At its founding dinner in May 1958, Kivie Kaplan and Jackie Robinson were honored. Adlai Stevenson was the featured speaker.

Several years later Kivie invested another $25,000 to help expand this work by the formation of M-REIT, the Mutual Real Estate Investment Trust, which now has about $40 million in assets.

Kivie was my very dear friend and sometimes my frank critic. I loved him dearly. His friendship and his criticism were both of tremendous value in strengthening the work that I am doing so that both blacks and whites and other minorities can live together.

# A Bridge between Communities

## James Farmer

ONE DAY in 1959, before the sit-ins and freedom rides and marches exploded onto the American scene, I sat in a cubbyhole at the NAACP headquarters where, for scarcely a week, I had been on staff bearing the rather non-committal title of "Activities Coordinator." An interloper in a maze of complicated interpersonal relationships within unfamiliar power equations, I sat alone, with some trepidation, puzzling.

The doorway was "darkened" by a smiling white face — rotund and friendly. "Welcome to a great organization, Jim," said Kivie Kaplan, with his hand extended. "I'm glad you're in the family and I know you're going to be a big help to us."

I had never met Kivie Kaplan before and did not know who he was until other staff members enlightened me. That one of the top officers of the NAACP Board of Directors would take time out to come by to offer encouragement to a new staff member and to make him feel at home was impressive enough. But more impressive was the total absence of any paternalism. And there was absolutely no question about his sincerity.

Even in that day a decade and a half ago — the heyday of interracialism in the civil rights movement — such relaxed empathy and unselfconscious identification were rare indeed.

It was a further measure of this man that in 1961, when I left the NAACP staff to become national director of CORE (Congress of Racial Equality), an organization which might have been considered a rival, he was one of the few of my

JAMES FARMER *is president of the Council on Minority Planning and Strategy.*

erstwhile associates who did not appear to consider it a betrayal of sorts. He wrote simply, "You're still in the family, Jim, because we're all fighting for the same cause. So I wish you luck." And the friendship and the communication never faltered.

Kivie did not stand in judgment when I committed what, to most of my liberal friends, was the unpardonable sin by becoming an HEW assistant secretary in the first Nixon Administration. Having despised Nixon for many years, Kivie must have had misgivings about the move; but he said only, "Good luck and I hope you're able to accomplish the things you're trying to do." And when I quit, less than two years later, Kivie sent congratulations.

No doubt the greatest strain in the Kivie Kaplan–civil rights love affair came when the Black Power motif exploded upon the civil rights movement. What for years had been a subtle undercurrent became a raging torrent, separating friends and setting aside old alliances.

Though it was primarily SNCC and secondarily CORE which led this new departure in 1966, the "young turks" of the NAACP, like most black youths, were swept up in it. Whites in SNCC were thrown out, and in CORE their role was made so untenable that they left.

Whites who had given blood and money felt turned upon and were puzzled. Kivie must have felt himself under siege as militant blacks with a growing self-awareness demanded a new agenda and total control.

I recall one occasion when I gave a lecture at a college in the Boston suburbs in 1968. Kivie and Emily joined me for dinner, as usual, and then drove me to the meeting. In the lecture I stressed the positive features of black pride, emphasizing its vast improvement over its precursor, "black self-hate." I sought to synthesize the best features of the old integrationism with those of the new black identity — within the context of an American cultural pluralism — unity through diversity — quoting Hillel's familiar words, "If I am not for myself. . . ."

Kivie, though no less friendly, no less compassionate, seemed a bit troubled throughout the talk. But his personal friendships were not even threatened by the tensions of that period, and he survived it as a top leader of the NAACP.

If he had a certain ambivalence on the new mood in the black community, so did most of us. The integration goals of the past were being refined, and perhaps redefined. And a redefinition of goals is always agonizing. But, because of his deep and abiding Jewishness, cultural pluralism was easier for him to understand than it was for many of our non-Jewish friends, for cultural identity has meant much to Jews all along and has now come to mean much to blacks as well.

Naturally, the transition has spawned excesses and absurdities in rhetoric. In all of this torrent, Kivie Kaplan's role became even more vital. For he was by virtue of his unique human qualities a bridge between two communities, once allies and now somewhat alienated and reaching for a new alliance and a new understanding.

That is the meaning of Kivie Kaplan. The smile was more than a slogan — it was also prophecy.

# A Passion for Social Justice

*Alfred Gottschalk*

FOR SOME years one has been hearing of a political drift to the right among Jews, an abandonment of or waning interest in the political liberalism and dedication to social justice and civil rights for which American Jews were so long and so honorably known. We live in a world of such rapid change that perhaps Jews are in the process of establishing new political and social priorities for themselves — but not every Jewish leader will find it in himself to greet the rumored rightward shift with much enthusiasm, and not every Jewish leader will be able to make his peace with such a shift. The late president of the Union of American Hebrew Congregations, Rabbi Maurice N. Eisendrath, was certainly not willing to give up the passionate advocacy of social justice which he believed central to Reform Judaism in America, and Rabbi Eisendrath had no stronger or more devoted supporter in this respect than Kivie Kaplan. For Kivie Kaplan, too, a Judaism — especially a Reform Judaism — in which social justice is relegated to the periphery was simply unthinkable.

His abiding concern for issues of conscience is so well known that it seems unnecessary to rehearse the lengthy list of his contributions to an America which views social justice and social action as nothing less than divine imperatives. His continued—one may say invincible—attachment to the National Association for the Advancement of Colored People was only one evidence of his concern. Another, of course, was the substantive support he gave the Kaplan Center for Religious Action in Washington, D.C., an agency rooted in the proposition that a Reform Judaism unresponsive to issues of social

---

RABBI ALFRED GOTTSCHALK *is president of*
*Hebrew Union College–Jewish Institute of Religion.*

justice is a mockery of itself. In short, if there is any reason to believe — and, given Kivie's wonderful *akshanut* (persistence) in this question, there would seem to be abundant reason to believe — that the American Jewish community and, in particular, its Reform element will resist the drift to the right which appears to be permeating the larger American society, Kivie Kaplan was in no small measure responsible. He was living testimony to the viability of social conscience among American Jews.

What was so splendid about all this is that Kivie Kaplan was no "professional" Jew. He was not a rabbi and would surely have been greatly embarrassed to hear himself described as a prophet. He was a man who had risen high in the world of American economic enterprise, but he never allowed his success in business to cloud his Jewish vision — his sense of himself as heir to a venerable and, so far as he was concerned, a vital tradition of Jewish love for justice. He was a man of humor and of sweetness for whom the world was a place of opportunity for doing good — in a quite direct and tangible way. Inspired by Jewish social ethics, he was determined to do all he could to demonstrate that the biblical injunction *tsedek tsedek tirdof* (justice is what you shall give yourself to) is not something for high-minded rumination; it is something a Jew takes with all the seriousness and activism he can, something a Jew makes a daily concern.

Jewish life in America has its weaknesses and its short-comings insofar as American social problems are concerned. Kivie Kaplan was not one of them. He was, on the contrary, exemplary for the *shiduch* (marriage) his life showed between sensitivity to social need and the teachings of the Reform synagogue. Maybe it is true that the American Jew is vanishing from the ranks of those devoted to social conscience, but, if Kivie Kaplan has had anything to say about it, the Jew dedicated to social justice will be a long, *long* time vanishing.

# 18

Kivie Kaplan and the
Union of American
Hebrew Congregations

*Alexander M. Schindler*

\*

AS THE editors of this *festschrift* will attest, I have had no little trouble in penning these lines. Not that material for an appreciation of Kivie Kaplan is lacking. His accomplishments, after all, were exceedingly great; their fruitage is rich and a boon to many — individuals and congregations alike. But I think now, rather, of the inner man and my response to him. These feelings cannot be encompassed by mere words; they are too great for that. Would that I were a musician. Then I could compose a song for him — a song without words, a song of faith and of love.

When I first met Kivie I thought him a rather simple man. His speech was plain, his presence not commanding. I well remember our first encounter. I had just been appointed the North East Council director for the UAHC, and I came to introduce myself. After we exchanged the customary courtesies, Kivie took my children by the hand and marched them to the basement of his Chestnut Hill home where a soda bar stood installed. He donned a white jacket and cap and began to dole out the ice cream, all the while explaining that when he was young he always wanted to be a soda jerk and never was and now, by God, that he could afford to be one, he *was* one. There was a twinkle in his eyes, responding to the delight of my girls. A boy in his middle teens joined us and Kivie casually explained that he was a Cuban youngster whom he chanced to meet and whom he had "adopted" to provide him a home. It was then that the process of revising my judgment of Kivie began. It was a process which had never really ended for our every meeting revealed a new dimension of his being. There was absolutely nothing that was simple about him. He was like a mountain lake, with depths which cannot be plumbed.

RABBI ALEXANDER SCHINDLER *is the president of the Union of American Hebrew Congregations and the chairman of the Conference of Presidents of Major American Jewish Organizations.*

I did not leave his house emptyhanded, then or ever since. And I received my first fistful of those "Keep Smiling" cards which became his hallmark.

Kivie left his mark wherever he went. Its impress, however, came from something more than print on paper. It came from a spirit within him and beyond him. It was fed by the flames of a fire which will never die.

What was his effect on that union of congregations in whose behalf I speak?

First and foremost, he was our conscience. Nothing morally shabby escaped his watchful concern. And when he saw a wrong he spoke his piece for justice, fearlessly yet softly, never in self-righteous anger, always insistent on those values which the world makes us forget.

His moral antennae were especially sensitive to power. He disdained its pomp and would not brook its abuse. He deemed power a trust, springing *from* the governed and existing *for* them. Those who hold it, therefore, are accountable for its exercise. No one is exempted from this accounting — neither the head of an institution, nor the ruler of people, nor even a tyrannical majority — indeed, the greater the power, the more potentially dangerous the abuse. Kivie stood with the Psalmist: absolute power belongs only to God.

Kivie's moral perceptions were rooted in the Jewish tradition. Certainly he did what he did out of an awareness of his Jewishness. He had internalized the ideal of *Kiddush ha-Shem*, sensing that whatever he did reflected upon his people and their faith. *Israel's* conscience was forged within the smithy of Kivie's soul.

Kivie thought and acted as a Jew always, but his concern embraced the world. This was the second area in which he made his impact on our union of congregations, in that he embodied the essential unity of the universal and the particular. His life gave lie to the notion that the two are somehow incompatible, that the service of the one precludes a devotion to the other. Jewishness mandates a concern for humankind —

so taught Kivie by example — nor can humankind be served by a Jew without a prior coming to terms with his Jewishness, without a continuing replenishing of that matrix, that enveloping element in which the Jew takes life and form.

And so, Kivie went about his way supporting just causes whatever be their label. When working for and among blacks, he did not hide his Jewishness; he wore it as a plume. He took no offense but pride when scurrilous articles and letters referred to him as a "nigger-loving Jew." And when narrow-minded Jews chided him to "worry about Jews and not Chicanos" he delighted to have me write them (his humility would not let him answer such letters himself) informing them just how much he had done for his people, had continued to do for them, here and in Israel, all over the world. The door of Kivie's heart was open to the world; but the post of that doorway was adorned with a *mezuzah*.

Lastly, and not in the least, the UAHC valued Kivie because the *individual* was at the end of his universe. He cared about each person and not just about people. Nothing was good to him that ignored the individual. No predatory collectivism for him, only and always *man*, not *men*! He would not let anyone be sacrificed for anything at all, not even for some presumed greater good. To see Kivie with someone who had fallen low was to see Kivie at his finest.

He gave the great gifts, publicly and properly so acclaimed. But he also gave much more: the hidden gift, deeds of human kindness known only to giver and to receiver and all the more precious for their tender privacy.

That was Kivie, but that was not the whole of him. There was one other element which went into his making which defined his essence. I speak of Emily, of course, of all earthly goods his most precious, who stood by his side, giving quiet assent to everything he did, bringing him grief only when she was not near. Emily, Kivie's wife — his love, his thought, his joy.

This volume has but one significance: to inspire us to

follow in his way. A midrash tells of a prince who was eager to have everyone know that he was the king's son. "Father," he cried out, "send messengers throughout the land to tell the people that I am your son, the son of the king!" And the king replied: "Would you really have the people know that you are the prince? Then put on my robes and crown and show the people how well you wear them." Even so does this *festschrift* speak to us. If we really want to share that crown which surrounds Kivie's name, why then we must also share that way which brought him honor. We must don the robe of righteousness and wear the crown of service which he so nobly bore.